NATURE IS THE WORST

500 REASONS YOU'LL NEVER WANT TO GO OUTSIDE AGAIN

NATURE IS THE WORST

E. REID ROSS

Adams Media
New York   London   Toronto   Sydney   New Delhi

Adams Media
An Imprint of Simon & Schuster, Inc.
57 Littlefield Street
Avon, Massachusetts 02322

For information about special discounts for bulk purchases, please contact Simon & Schuster Special Sales at 1-866-506-1949 or business@simonandschuster.com.

The Simon & Schuster Speakers Bureau can bring authors to your live event. For more information or to book an event contact the Simon & Schuster Speakers Bureau at 1-866-248-3049 or visit our website at www.simonspeakers.com.

Interior images © Clipart.com; insima/123RF

Manufactured in the United States of America

10 9 8 7 6 5 4 3 2

Library of Congress Cataloging-in-Publication Data has been applied for.

ISBN 978-1-4405-9907-1
ISBN 978-1-4405-9908-8 (ebook)

CONTENTS

For McMac, Joefoozle, Minky, Madre,
and all my Yodas at Cracked.com

INTRODUCTION

A lot of people will tell you that "getting in touch with nature" is something every-one should do. What they fail to mention is that every time you leave the comforts of civilization, Mother Nature might just be the one getting in touch with *you*. And her preferred method of saying "howdy" is usually by way of fang, lightning bolt, or uticating hair.

This book isn't designed as a justification for staying inside and playing more video games, or to scare everyone who reads it into surrounding their property with a kerosene moat. In fact, the average person may never have to face (or find attached to his or her face) the myriad horrors that dwell within these pages. But the public should be aware that they exist—everywhere, all the time, and hopefully not right behind you.

Through many hours of meticulous research (and the occasional shot to steel my nerves), I have compiled a formidable collection of the living nightmares that call our planet home. From the depths of the ocean, where squid have the most nightmarish sex imaginable, to suburban swimming pools that could be filled with amoebas just waiting to feast on your brain. From the primeval forests, replete with wanton ape orgies, to the deserts, where spiders cartwheel like tiny, ghoul-ish Mary Lou Rettons across the dunes. The conclusion I've reached is that there are few, if any, habitats on Earth that are completely free from disturbing natural behavior. The creatures compiled here range from the massive to the microscopic, and may well be lurking in the very bathroom where you're sitting right now.

So sit back and . . . well, maybe not relax, but at least calm down a little in order to take in the information that follows with a clear head. Because there's always the possibility that you *are* going to encounter one of the organisms men-tioned in this book during your lifetime. And it might be nice to know, the next time you're taking a hike, what exactly that thing is that's burrowing into your arm to deposit its payload of eggs. Godspeed!

CHAPTER 1

Denizens of the Deep and Lurkers of the Lakes

The peaceful feeling that comes over you while looking out over a gorgeous sea vista or tranquil lake is a lie—a damn, dirty lie. Danger lurks not just at the ocean's surface, where deadly jellyfish bob, or solely at the bottom, where Stygian horrors skulk in the depths. From top to bottom, 71 percent of the Earth's surface is a carnival of brutality, and freshwater provides little respite. And during the rare moments when the life forms that call the water home aren't engaged in a maelstrom of violence, you can rest assured they're doing something gross, such as . . .

Sperm whales (*Physeter macrocephalus*) and their diminutive cousins, pygmy sperm whales (*Kogia breviceps*), are able to store large quantities of fecal matter in reserve for emergencies. When threatened, they will release it suddenly and disappear behind a massive cloud that divers have described as a "poonado."

I guess scientists had a tough choice between "jizz whales" and "poop ninjas."

> ❯ "Sperm Whale's Emergency Evacuation . . . of Its Bowels," *New Scientist*, newscientist. com

Fishing for sharks, cutting off their fins for soup, and then throwing the rest back into the sea is a hideous practice, but the sharks may be getting the last laugh. Researchers at the University of Miami found out in 2012 that shark fins contain a neurotoxin that scientists have linked to Lou Gehrig's disease and other degenerative conditions, such as Alzheimer's.

Which finally explains why Gehrig left no money to his family and instead donated everything to The Society for the Furtherance of Shark Mutilation.

> ❯ "BMAA Neurotoxin Found in Shark Fins Linked to Alzheimer's Disease," *Asian Scientist*, asianscientist.com

In terms of squid sex, the giant squid (genus *Architeuthis*) must overcome a big problem in regard to the females' lack of proper lady-parts. Not to be deterred, these squid take a direct route, and just repeatedly stab the females with their hooked tentacles and parrot-like beaks. Once a male has brutalized a female to where there's a sizeable enough hole in her body, he then inseminates the wound.

And here I thought the furries, Bronies, and Germans already had the market cornered on disturbing coitus.

> ❯ "When Giant Squids Mate, It's a Stab in the Dark," *New York Times*, nytimes.com; "Sex Trap for Giant Squid," BBC News, bbc.co.uk

Since female greater hooked squid (*Onykia ingens*) don't have much in the way of vaginas, the males require an outside-the-box way of inseminating them. To compensate for the females' lack of proper lady-parts, the males deploy flesh-dissolving sperm. Once their little squirmers find purchase on a female, the spermatophores proceed to independently burrow their way inside her body, and continue to bore their way through until they find something to fertilize.

Which just goes to show that there's some truth in that old children's rhyme, "When squid fellatio's what you crave, a dental dam your life might save."

> "Bizarre Squid Sex Techniques Revealed," *National Geographic*, nationalgeographic.com

Irukandji jellyfish live in many places, from the coasts of Australia to a recent infiltration of the Florida Keys, and they're both the smallest and most venomous jellyfish in the world. On a scale of 0–10, experts report the pain from their sting to be a 40. In addition, one of the side effects of the sting, apart from all the abdominal pain, nausea, and vomiting, is "a feeling of impending doom."

> "Jellyfish Gone Wild!" National Science Foundation, nsf.com; "Apparently There's a Jellyfish Whose Sting Causes Feelings of Impending Doom," *New York*, nymag.com

---

That's some pretty intense pain, considering that watching Steven Seagal's entire filmography is only considered to be around a 35.

On the opposite end of the jellyfish size spectrum are *Cyanea capillata*, or lion's mane jellyfish. The most outrageously monstrous specimen of this particular species, which washed up on the Massachusetts Bay shore in 1870, measured 7 feet across and had 120-foot tentacles. Pretty impressive for a beast without a heart or a brain. It's entirely possible that there are bigger lion's mane jellyfish out there, and we can probably safely assume that they can kill you just as horribly as the smaller ones can.

What's even more shocking is to see a creature so huge, squishy, and dangerous so far from an Arkansas gun show.

> "Giant Jellyfish: Arctic Lion's Mane (*Cyanea capillata*)," *Extreme Science*, extremescience.com

Moray eels of the family Muraenidae have a set of secondary jaws, just like the monsters in the *Alien* movies, which they use to drag live prey into their throats after biting them. These pharyngeal jaws remove the need to expand their mouths to laboriously gulp down a meal, so it's actually a much more practical system than the movie version. It allows the eels to devour victims much larger than themselves, while they remain hidden in the dark crevasses in which they dwell.

Which might explain why so many lost divers' last known words were, "That's it, man. Game over, man. Game over!"

> "Moray Eels Grab Prey with 'Alien' Jaws," *National Geographic*, nationalgeographic.com

Speaking of the *Alien* movies, remember how the queen had those freaky, glass-like teeth? Go figure, there's a type of moray eel that has an even more intimidating mouth full of nightmares. The fangtooth moray (*Enchelycore anatina*) has two rows of inexplicably semi-transparent teeth, on both the upper and lower jaws, that make the eel's face look like a meaty cavern full of icicles.

❯ "Fangtooth Moray Eel," Fish Laboratory, fishlaboratory.com

Until they kill something of course, at which point they look like the world's most hazardous cherry-flavored popsicles.

When you think of catfish, the first word that comes to mind probably isn't *man-eater*. Nonetheless, there have been numerous reports worldwide of gigantic bewhiskered scum suckers gulping down unwary humans—from claims that the South American piraiba loves to swallow fishermen whole, to accusations that India's giant goonch has developed a taste for man flesh after feasting on the discarded remains of funeral pyre corpses. These stories are anecdotal and should be taken with a grain of salt, but what isn't under debate is the reality that catfish can sometimes grow as large as grizzly bears—and that a good number of them have spines on their fins that can deliver venom like a goddamn cobra.

❯ "Killer Catfish? Venomous Species Surprisingly Common, Study Finds," Michigan News, University of Michigan, ns.umich.edu

Combine all that with how they love pretending to be sexy singles looking for love on Facebook, and you have a potential threat that only a fool would ignore.

Somewhere on Earth, right now, there may be a 200-foot worm. They're hard to accurately measure, being squirmy worms, but the longest species of marine ribbon worm (phylum Nemertea) is believed to stretch longer than a blue whale, making it one of the longest animals on the planet. And thanks to their ability to regenerate, if you cut one in half that just means you have two 100-foot worms.

❯ "14 Fun Facts about Marine Ribbon Worms," *Smithsonian*, smithsonianmag.com

Now if we could just get one of these things on some sort of giant hook, we can finally start fishing for Cthulhu.

The giant oarfish (*Regalecus glesne*), a deep-water monstrosity that can sprawl out to over 36 feet long, looks like a silvery Christmas ribbon crossed with a parrot and can survive being cut in half—more than half actually. These bony fish can "self-amputate" up to 75 percent of their bodies in order to escape predators. And when they're sick and/or dying, they'll often float up to the surface and just wait to croak like an underfed goldfish in a bowl. Which is why they're believed to be the source of many ancient sea serpent legends.

❯"The 28-Foot Sea Monster That Can Survive Being Cut in Half," *Wired*, wired.com

The "oar" in their name comes from how they're so thin and long like . . . an oar. Nope, no need at all to reference how people used to think they were monsters. Way to be creative, people.

Eating sushi can be hazardous, especially if it's the "fugu" variety, which is made from the raw flesh of the various species of highly poisonous pufferfish. The smallest mistake in preparation can leave the person who eats it completely paralyzed while still totally aware of what's happening around him or her. Eventually the paralysis makes its way to the major organs, at which point an expensive meal turns into death by asphyxiation. And if you simply can't resist the temptation and decide to order this dish despite all the dangers, you might want to tell the chef to "hold the ovaries," since that's the part of the fish that is particularly toxic.

That didn't stop a famous Kabuki performer named Bando Mitsugoro VIII from acting like a tough guy and ordering a plate full of fugu livers. They say his death scene was very realistic.

❯"Fugu: The Fish More Poisonous Than Cyanide," BBC News, bbc.com

One might assume that the corpulent manatee (genus *Trichechus*) isn't a particularly agile creature, and probably just floats in place all day—at the most perhaps flapping its humongous paddle-tail occasionally to lumber along to the next area where it can loll around like a fatass. But all three species of "sea cows" can actually control their vertical movements with just as much precision as any svelte sea lion. And they don't even have to move at all to accomplish this feat, because they do it by controlling their farts.

Which is why when experts tell you not to eat an hour before swimming, they're not accounting for the advantages provided by burritos.

> ❯ "Florida Manatee, *Trichechus manatus latirostrus*," Florida Oceanographic Society, floridaocean.org

The spectacularly weird mantis shrimp (order Stomatopoda) has a number of disconcerting qualities, but the most alarming may be its ability to punch harder than a *Pacific Rim* Kaiju (relative to size, of course). This shrimp's uppercut can devastate anything that so much as looks at it funny with the power of a .22-caliber bullet. Their furious claw-fists shoot out with such velocity that it actually creates a small flash of light from the heat. And if you're one of those weirdos who thinks keeping something like that in a home aquarium sounds like a good plan, you'd better be able to afford a bulletproof tank, because it's more than capable of smashing the glass.

> ❯ "Shrimp Spring into Shattering Action," *USA Today*, usatoday.com

And then presumably come crawling out to deliver some sweet chin music, in payment for the naive and foolish belief that a punk like you would be capable of containing their unbound rage.

If you had to guess, how long would you say "the immortal jellyfish" lives? Did you just say "forever"? Okay, I suppose that was pretty obvious. Maybe I should have started that off with the scientific name. Anyway, it's true. *Turritopsis dohrnii* jellyfish get old and/or injured just like everyone else, but before death can come knocking, they can somehow render themselves down to a primordial goop and replicate themselves into a swarm of identical clones. Essentially, they're impossible to kill.

❯ "The Immortal Jellyfish," American Museum of Natural History, amnh.org

---

That sounds like a challenge to me. How about we arm them with little swords, convince them they're Scottish aliens from the planet Zeist, and tell them, "There can be only one!"

You've surely heard of electric eels (*Electrophorus electricus*), but something you maybe weren't aware of is that they're not eels at all. They're actually more closely related to catfish. And you also might not have heard about the way they have to regularly come up to the surface (or flop onto land) to take gulps of air, which is just plain creepy for some reason. The majority of the cells in this freshwater fish's body are dedicated to the whole electricity thing, and they can deliver a shock of up to 600 volts. For reference, that's 50 times the power in the average car battery. And although electric eel shocks don't often kill directly, the stun factor has caused several people to drown.

So, if you're suicidal and have a heart condition, you could always jump on a plane and try for one of the most spectacular epitaphs of all time: "Tased by some asshole fish in the Amazon."

❯ "Electric Eel," Eden, eden.uktv.co.uk

Sharks have some of the most disturbing, seemingly H.R. Giger–inspired eggs in the animal kingdom. But it turns out the babies who get to begin their lives inside eggs are the lucky ones, at least compared to the pups of the sand tiger shark (*Carcharias taurus*). The offspring of this species are born live and start out much larger and stronger than other sharks—and that's because out of a litter of twelve, only two sharks ever emerge from the womb. The largest one devours every single other fetus, except for one, while still in utero.

Which presumably means you're going to get one shark that is very well-fed, and another that is very polite.

❯ "Why Shark Embryos Eat Each Other Up in Utero," Seeker, seeker.com

Thanks to G-rated movies and an ability to soak onlookers on command, killer whales (*Orcinus orca*) have enjoyed a rather undeserved reputation for being genial giants. The reality is that these whales were given their homicidally ominous name for a reason, and they are capable of engaging in acts of wanton, heartless cruelty. Seals are frequently the targets of their unrelenting bullying, and killer whales have been known to "play" with them (in the cat-and-mouse sense) for hours before the eventual dismemberment. One favorite game is to play "catch" with the seals, by punting them out of the water and 80 feet into the air.

❯ "7 Reasons Killer Whales Are Evil Geniuses," *The Atlantic*, theatlantic.com

Seals have a name for terror—and it's Willy. Also Shamu, probably. And Tilikum from the documentary **Blackfish** *is basically Michael Myers.*

The waters surrounding Florida have been invaded by not one but two species of flamboyant and outrageously poisonous lionfish. It's gotten so bad that many consider these fish "the most destructive exotic species" in that area of the country (and that's saying something, considering they're competing with boa constrictors and foot-long snails for that honor). Both the red lionfish (*Pterois volitans*) and the common lionfish (*Pterois miles*) have voracious appetites and are rapidly eating every other local fish to the point of extinction. So, being the adaptable sort of fish that they are, the lionfish are now eating themselves.

❯"This Beautiful But Destructive Fish Is Resorting to Cannibalism," *National Geographic*, nationalgeographic.com

Thus creating the perfect snorkeling destination for those who like their scenic grandeur served with a healthy dose of existential horror.

Just about all crabs have built-in weaponry,

and of course I'm talking about their grasping, sometimes ridiculously oversized claws. But while most crabs are quite happy defending themselves via the power of pinch, a couple species decided they needed an upgrade. Oddly enough, they also happen to be arguably the two least intimidatingly named crustaceans in the sea. The pom pom (*Lybia edmondsoni*) and teddy bear (*Polydectus cupulifer*) crabs have learned to snatch tiny, stinging sea anemones in their claws, and wave them around like menacing little pieces of flair whenever danger presents itself.

The biggest threat to the pom pom crab may be the "quarterback fish," a flashy parasite that impregnates young crabs before their prime, causing them to give up their dreams and spend the rest of their lives wondering what could have been.

❯"*Polydectus cupulifer*, a member of Round Crabs (Family Xanthidae)" iNaturalist, inaturalist.org

The head of the barreleye (also called the "spook fish") looks like an aquarium filled with nightmares. It's completely transparent, allowing anyone in the vicinity to get a clear view of the barreleye's brain, internal ocular structures, and whatever the hell else is going on in there. Reportedly this setup allows them to better look upwards at prey, which does nothing to explain why the scientific name of the family to which these fish belong is Opisthoproctidae, which is a combination of the Greek words for "behind" and "anus."

> "Researchers Solve Mystery of Deep-Sea Fish with Tubular Eyes and Transparent Head," Monterey Bay Aquarium Research Institute, mbari.org

Maybe it refers to how these fish are so alien-looking that the people who discovered them were terrified that they were about to receive a rectal probe?

Urechis unicinctus is a species of marine spoon worm more widely known as the fat innkeeper worm or, less flatteringly, the penis fish or sea penis. The "innkeeper" name came about because they dig tunnels that other animals use for shelter. Those other names refer to how they look like pulsating, uncircumcised schlongs. Which seems to be doing little to prevent people in some parts of the world from eating them raw. And sometimes . . . alive and squirming.

> "Penis Fish (*Urechis unicinctus*)," iNaturalist, inaturalist.org

The problem with eating sea penis is that a half hour later you're hungry again. You know, for more sea penis.

The ancient and hideous frilled shark (*Chlamydoselachus anguineus*) is one of the most primitive species of living sharks, and they have row upon row of three-pronged, needle-like teeth that look like little flowers. It's believed the weird configuration actually lures prey into their mouths, fooling fish into thinking the teeth are something tasty to eat. Long story short: they're not.

> "Frilled Shark (*Chlamydoselachus anguineus*)," Wildscreen Arkive, arkive.org

You may never have heard the phrase, "Beware of sharks bearing gifts." Probably because it's so goddamn obvious.

If you happen to be hungry enough to start eating fish heads, you should stay away from a species of sea bream called *Sarpa salpa*, because eating their heads can lead to ichthyoallyeinotoxism. Or you could describe the condition in a more fun way: hallucinogenic fish poisoning. The experience isn't very far off from an LSD high, but one big difference is that instead of an effect that lasts for just hours, a case of ichthyoallyeinotoxism will have you tripping for days.

❯"Hallucinogenic Foods," *Guardian*, theguardian.com

So what fun is it pelting dirty boardwalk hippies with fish heads if it turns out they actually enjoy it?

Nobody should have to tell you that sharks can be dangerous, but the bull shark (*Carcharhinus leucas*) is a special breed of treacherous. Regarded by many experts as the most vicious fish on the planet, they also have the strongest bite of all sharks and will occasionally wander into fresh water to sink their teeth into human swimmers. It's a little puzzling as to exactly why bull sharks have such strong jaws, which are stronger than needed to kill and eat most prey. But researchers suspect it's helpful for cracking open turtles like a walnut.

❯"Bull Sharks Have Strongest Bite of All Shark Species," BBC, bbc.co.uk; "Bull Shark Threat: They Swim Where We Swim," *National Geographic*, nationalgeographic.com

One emerging theory is as simple as it is obvious: Bull sharks are dicks.

A fish called a stargazer sounds like it must be something beautiful and delicate. The reality is that the family of fish that somehow got this title (Uranoscopidae) is an abominable combination of various childhood nightmares. And not only do stargazers look like angry blobs of toothy hatred, but they're also venomous and can shock with an electrical charge to boot. Their preferred modus operandi is to lie under the sand and ambush passing fish by chomping on their faces. Oh, and in case you were wondering, the only reason they're called stargazers is because their eyes are on top of their heads to allow them to peek out from their hiding places.

And not, in fact, because they make those who discover their existence immediately want to become astronauts to get as far away from them as possible.

❯ "The Stargazer Fish Is Seriously Weird," Azula, Azula.com

Imagine one of those cute, roly-poly pillbugs you've seen crawling around in your garden. Now imagine one that's 2½-feet long, and you'll get a good idea of what a giant isopod is. Although there are numerous species of them in the genus *Bathynomus*, you'll probably never find one in your backyard, thankfully. They lurk in the dark depths of the sea, hundreds of feet down, where they feast mainly on the corpses of whales and just about any other disgusting dead thing that doesn't have the decency to float.

Up until the late 1980s, it was believed a major part of the giant isopod's diet included gambling enthusiasts who didn't pay their debts to the Mafia in a timely manner.

❯ "Shocking Giant Isopod Rises from the Abyss," Reef Builders, reefbuilders.com

If you're ever vacationing at a tropical resort and submit to the urge to swim with dolphins, you should be very wary if one of them tries to lead you toward some secluded cove for a little one-on-one interaction. Because that squeaky son of a bitch may be trying to rape you. Male dolphins have absolutely committed sexual assaults on humans, and they're pretty indiscriminate about which gender they'll try to penetrate. The mechanics alone might make such an unspeakable act seem impossible, but these chattering perverts have both the equipment and the inclination to get the job done. Female dolphins apparently aren't averse to this sort of arrangement either, at least if you believe the man who wrote an entire book about a torrid, six-month romantic relationship he enjoyed with a dolphin named Dolly.

❯"Can Dolphins Rape Humans?" *Washington City Paper,* washingtoncitypaper.com

The author also admitted to having a similarly conjugal relationship with a dog. But I suppose after they broke up he may have taken his friends' advice too literally when they told him, "It's okay, man. There are plenty of fish in the sea."

A further example of egregious dolphin malfeasance is how they're the only known marine creatures that kill other species just for kicks. "Baby shark volleyball" is one game they'll play for mortified onlookers, a pastime which involves the dolphins repeatedly launching the juvenile fish high into the air until it is battered into oblivion. Even their fellow cetaceans aren't immune to their murderously cruel tomfoolery, as porpoises are also targets for the dolphin's "games." Porpoises have been found washed up on shore, clearly pummeled to death for no other reason than some dolphin's sick pleasure at watching them die.

❯"Research: Dolphins Play 'Shark Volleyball,'" UPI, upi.com; "Dolphin Serial Killers?" *New Scientist,* newscientist.com

Do you suppose that all the "talking" Flipper did was merely his concerted attempt to lure those kids into some underwater, windowless van?

The mating call of the plainfin midshipman fish (*Porichthys notatus*) is a loud, droning hum that's clearly audible from shore and has been compared to the sound of chanting monks or a didgeridoo (that weird Australian horn thing that's popular among Aborigines and burnouts). This exuberantly horny species of toadfish can produce such a racket that the noise has been known to keep entire cities awake, and their incessant moaning has even been blamed for a number of suicides.

If you've ever spent any time in a coed college dorm, I'm sure you can relate.

❯ *"What Is the Truth Behind Spooky Bristol Hum?" Daily Express,* express.co.uk

Sea lice, who cause a rash known as "seabather's eruption," thankfully aren't an oceangoing version of the verminous scourge of grade-schoolers everywhere. It's a term that instead describes when tiny baby jellyfish gather together en masse and collectively sting anyone foolish enough to enter their domain. Symptoms include rashy bumps, a flu-like fever, headache, nausea, and chills. It's merely one of the troubling circumstances that can befall you whenever you go swimming in the Caribbean or other tropical locations. Florida waters experienced a troubling outbreak as recently as the summer of 2016.

❯ *"'Sea Lice' Are Actually Not-So-Cute Baby Jellyfish," CNN,* cnn.com

As a side note, "seabather's eruption" can also describe the syndrome wherein a snorkeler, minding his own business, suddenly turns around and notices that there's a shark approaching.

The largest bony fish in the world is the monstrous ocean sunfish (*Mola mola*). They can weigh more than 2½ tons and look like a massive floating head with wings. Sunfish females also produce more eggs than any other known vertebrate, and can squirt out 3 million in a single session. Both genders are so creepy to look at that one has to wonder how they got such a pleasant name. But in fact, the "sun" part has nothing to do with the way they look but rather refers to their odd habit of lying on their sides at the water's surface, which makes it appear to onlookers as if they're sunbathing (or dead).

While they're floating up there like sick goldfish, seabirds will often land nearby and pick the parasites off their flesh. It has yet to be conclusively determined whether this is an example of a symbiotic relationship between fish and birds or merely some kind of sick perversion.

> "Mola Mola: The Weirdest Fish in the Ocean?" The Nature Conservancy, nature.org

If a shark with a chainsaw for a head sounds like something you'd only see in a drawing that a creative but troubled twelve-year-old might produce for his therapist, then you're obviously not familiar with the sawfish. The family (Pristidae) includes several species of such a fish that live throughout the world, including Florida. These abominations can live in both the ocean and freshwater, have the bodies of sharks (they're actually rays), and can grow up to 18 feet long. The lumberjack equipment on their faces is used for thrashing through the water to incapacitate (a more appropriate word would probably be *mutilate*) entire schools of fish at once. They're generally considered harmless to humans, though, unless provoked.

Which obviously includes drunkenly pulling them out of the water, pretending to pull a starter cord, and going, "Vroom vroom!" That probably won't end well.

> "Sharp Teeth Make Sawfish Dangerous," *Orlando Sentinel*, orlandosentinel.com; "Smalltooth Sawfish (*Pristis pectinata*)," Wildscreen Arkive, arkive.org

Herring (family Clupeidae) communicate with one another through the power of farts. When these diminutive prey fish are gliding around in their massive schools of thousands, they're able to effectively coordinate their movements by way of "a variety of whistles and thumps." Researchers were initially confused as to what these sounds were, until they eventually figured out that it was fishy flatulence.

❯"Farting Fish Keep in Touch," *Science*, sciencemag.org

Which is pretty much the same way my grandfather used to signal the end of conversations at family functions.

Finding a crab or a lobster in one's pants wouldn't be on many people's list of favorite beachside happenstances, but at least those crustaceans aren't venomous. Hell yes they are! Or at least one is. In 2013 experts discovered the first crustacean (a species of remipede that looks like a centipede, in case you'd like to make a children's rhyme out of it) able to pump you full of a paralyzing agent by way of a spiderish fang. Also like a spider, the venom of the newly named *Speleonectes tulumensis* liquefies the innards of its prey, making it easier to suck out through the fang holes.

❯"First Venomous Crustacean Found," BBC, bbc.com

They actually spend most of their time lurking in underwater caves, so watch out when you're down in the oceanic depths. Then again, if you count "deep-sea cave spelunking" among your list of hobbies, you probably won't have a very long life anyway.

The blobfish (*Psychrolutes marcidus*) became Internet-famous a few years ago when its lumpy, cartoonish visage went viral. However, the story behind its goofy appearance is actually pretty gross. The flesh of a blobfish is very gelatinous, which is helpful for its movement in the high-pressure, deep-water environment in which it lives. In fact it looks pretty normal down there. But when one is brought to the surface, the pressure change basically turns it into a sad, melty glob of snot.

❯"Meet the Blobfish," Discovery, discovery.com

For all we know they're still perfectly delicious, so next time you're at a sushi restaurant, try ordering the "loogie roll."

The pacu, a South American freshwater fish that's related to piranhas, has teeth that look disturbingly like they belong in a human mouth. As off-putting as that looks, one at can least take comfort in the fact that these fish aren't the flesh-decimating carnivores that their cousins are. However, as their teeth are great for cracking open nuts and seeds, rumor has it that the pacu will sometimes chomp a man's testicles clean off. This claim may be completely unfounded hearsay, but it's pretty hard to discount something like that out of hand. Especially since they've recently been sighted in New Jersey.

›"Invasive Pacu Fish with Human-Like Teeth Found in New Jersey," *National Geographic*, nationalgeographic.com

It's a shame that they didn't show up fifteen years ago, when they could have made a cameo on The Sopranos *in an episode called, "Bada Bing, Bada Bish, Holy Crap My Stugots Just Got Chewed Off by a Goddamn Fish."*

Remember that poor neglected hermit crab that spent its mercifully short life trying to scratch its way out of your grade-school class terrarium? Well, there's a version out there that's 9 pounds and 3 feet across. The coconut crab (*Birgus latro*) is so named because its unspeakably huge claws are capable of cracking coconuts, and it's quite possible that it ate Amelia Earhart.

›"Coconut Crabs Eat Everything from Kittens to, Maybe, Amelia Earhart," *Smithsonian*, smithsonianmag.com

So if you're ever shipwrecked on one of the deserted islands in the Pacific or Indian Ocean where these things live, it might be in your best interest to avoid mentioning how you painted little nail polish rainbows and smiley faces on Mr. Pinchy.

The vaguely pornographic-sounding black swallower (*Chiasmodon niger*) is a species of deep-sea fish that got its name for a very good reason. First off, they're black. But aside from that, they can swallow down objects that are twice their length and ten times their mass. To accomplish this feat, they obviously have ridiculously large mouths. And within those mouths are sharp, backward-facing teeth on both the jaws and the palate, which aid in forcing their wriggling prey down into the swallower's expandable stomach (which hangs below the fish like a garbage bag). However, sometimes even a fish known for swallowing can bite off more than it can chew, and the gases from an especially oversized, decomposing meal can cause its whole digestive system to explode.

Just imagine what a fearsome creature it'll be once it finally evolves the ability to fart.

❯ "The Black Swallower,"
Australian Geographic,
australiangeographic.com.au

The legs of the Japanese spider crab (*Macrocheira kaempferi*) are thought to measure up to 12 feet long. It's basically a walking case of arachnophobia. A 5-foot long specimen was discovered in 2010 and was dubbed "Crabzilla." The beast was not in fact destroyed by the Japanese military during a rampage through downtown Tokyo but rather taken on a European tour, much to the horror of children across the continent.

Nonetheless, Crabzilla must have been grateful, seeing as how if the tour had taken place in Japan, the last stop would have been a date with a dash of wasabi.

❯ "Crabzilla! At 5 Feet Tall, Biggest Known Crab Heads to U.K.," Treehugger, treehugger.com

Even at the bottom of the ocean there is no escape from the scourge of spiders. And while sea spiders aren't true arachnids, they're about as close as you can get, evolution-wise, without actually being one. There are well over 1,000 species of them, and they range in size from minuscule to tarantula-sized. One difference between sea spiders and true spiders is the fact that a few varieties possess an even greater abundance of spindly legs (10–12), and those horrid appendages just so happen to be the place they house their genitalia. The way they eat is right in line with the standard spider's preference for the gruesome, however, as their hunting strategy consists mainly of stabbing their proboscises into soft-fleshed invertebrates and sucking out their insides. After which everything is digested in, again, their legs.

❭"The Giant Sea Spider That Sucks Life Out of Its Prey," *New Scientist*, newscientist.com

---

There has to be at least one story of a man who became a pirate due to his severe arachnophobia, lost his life at sea, and then arrived at Davy Jones's locker only to see a bunch of spiders scuttling around. Upon which his doomed soul would go on to moan for all eternity, "You gotta be shittin' me."

Sea cucumbers aren't the most agile or fearsome of creatures, so in order to defend themselves from attack they need to think outside the box. And what could be more outside the box than spewing your internal organs out of your anus? This method apparently works, and is helped by the fact that their innards are not just stringy, sticky, and toxic, but they're also retrievable after being expelled. Oh, and this disconcerting process is also how sea cucumbers eat.

You have our sincerest apologies if you were eating a salad, enjoying a pickle, or relaxing with a cucumber facial immediately prior to this discussion.

❭"Sea Cucumber's Self-Evisceration," Adam Savage's Tested, tested.com

The naval shipworm (*Teredo navalis*) is actually a type of saltwater clam, but they don't spend their lives cowering in shells, waiting to be bashed into pulp by some jerk of a sea otter. The way these clams earned their nautical nickname was by becoming the bane of sailors everywhere, thanks to their propensity for chewing holes in the hulls of wooden boats and causing millions of dollars worth of damage every year (according to historical records they nearly sank two of Christopher Columbus's ships). That's why another term that's used in reference to these clams is *termites of the sea.*

> "Termite of the Sea's Wood Destruction Strategy Revealed," Joint Genome Institute, United States Department of Energy, jgi.doe.gov

And you wouldn't believe how expensive things get when an exterminator starts charging for things like scuba gear, shark repellant, and barnacle rash ointment.

In most encounters with a shark, it's the teeth that present the major cause for concern. However, there's one shark that whips its opponents into submission like a hateful farmer with an extraordinarily disrespectful mule, well before any biting comes into play. All four species of thresher shark (genus *Alopias*) have "scythe-like" tails that are as long as their bodies, and what they do with them isn't suitable for family viewing. They can snap the tips through the water at speeds of up to 80 miles per hour, and when it comes in contact with another fish the result is as if it had been in a head-on collision with a whirling Cuisinart.

> "Thresher Sharks Hunt with Huge Weaponized Tails," *National Geographic*, nationalgeographic.com

Excuse me for a moment while I get myself together. I just had a flashback to an unfortunate high school gym locker room towel-snapping incident.

The mummichog cannot be stopped. Also known as mummies, gudgeons, and mud minnows (and scientifically as *Fundulus heteroclitus*), this species of killifish can survive in practically any environment, including those that would normally, um . . . kill a fish. They can be transferred from freshwater to the saltiest of saltwater with no ill effects, laugh in the face of many toxic chemicals, and can even withstand being sent up into the vacuum of space. Which scientists did in 1973 for some reason, and which revealed that mummichogs can swim just fine in zero gravity.

❯ "The Toughest Fish on Earth . . . and in Space," *New Scientist*, newscientist.com

Finally, a fish that might actually survive longer than a month in the average child's home aquarium.

However, there's one place where even the mighty mummichog can't hack it: underwater volcanoes. But there's an abhorrent-looking species of tongue-fish that can. *Symphurus thermophilus* love to scamper and frolic (as much as a creature that looks like a wet cow pie with fins is able) across pools of molten sulfur. And they are somehow able to tolerate temperatures as hot as 180 degrees Celsius in the acidic water near hydrothermal vents like it ain't nothin' but a thang.

❯ "Fish Dance on Sulphur Cauldrons," BBC, bbc.co.uk

So we have a creature named after a tongue that likes to hang out where it's stinky and hot. It's a damn shame when nature feels like it has to emulate Penthouse Forum just to get attention from the scientific community.

Geographic cone snails (*Conus geographus*) are so preposterously poisonous that they're colloquially known as "cigarette snails." Not because these Indo-Pacific mollusks will slowly give you cancer over the course of several decades, but because when one stings you, you'll have somewhere in the area of five minutes (the approximate time it takes to smoke a Marlboro loosey) before the venom kills you.

❯ "Beautiful but Deadly Cone Snails," *Asbury Park Press*, app.com

Thus inspiring another nickname: "The amount of time it takes for the average filmgoer to walk out of a Rob Schneider movie" snail.

The Bobbit worm (*Eunice aphroditois*) has been described as "the ocean's most disturbing predator," and for numerous reasons. First it's a 10-foot, carnivorous worm, which should be enough to earn the title right there. But then there's the fact that they look like something out of a low-budget sci-fi movie that may or may not star Kevin Bacon, have a hunting style that's essentially "lunge and snap fish in half," and are incongruously colorful in a way you'd expect only if H.P. Lovecraft had made a living designing snake piñatas. And then there's this: There's a very real possibility that the Bobbit worm may have been named after Lorena Bobbitt, the woman who famously chopped off her husband's penis in a fit of rage.

I sincerely hope that's true, if for no other reason than so future generations of Bobbitts won't be doomed forever to be associated solely with that "incident," along with John Wayne Bobbitt's subsequent porno career.

❯ "10-Foot Bobbit Worm Is the Ocean's Most Disturbing Predator," *Wired*, wired.com; "*Eunice aphroditois* Is Rainbow, Terrifying," *Scientific American*, scientificamerican.com

You may remember the barracuda as that bastard of a fish that killed Nemo's mom. And with jaws lined with saw-like teeth that operate like scissors (which effectively slice whatever they chomp down on completely in half), the members of the genus *Sphyraena* can obviously pose a threat to humans as well. Some divers fear barracudas even more than sharks, due in part to their disconcerting penchant for stalking. Not to mention the fact that the aftermath of an attack is a little different in terms of gruesomeness than what you could expect from an encounter with a great white. Possibly the only reason barracuda-related fatalities are rare is because they prefer one-time hit-and-run attacks over lengthy maulings.

And furthermore, barracudas have an awesome classic Heart song named after them, while great whites only got some crappy hair metal band from the '80s.

❯ "Great Barracuda," Florida Museum of Natural History, flmnh. ufl.edu; *Dive/First Responder* by Richard A. Clinchy

There are only a few select fish that have had the honor of starring in their very own Syfy original movie, and the northern snakehead (*Channa argus*) has the distinction of having been in several. But after their invasion of America's waterways, it was probably well deserved. Dubbed the "Frankenfish" by the media, these amply fanged malignancies were found in a pond in Maryland, causing a brief panic on the East Coast of the United States. The public's fear was only exacerbated when it came to light that snakeheads can breathe for long periods of time outside the water, enabling them to wriggle and flop their way over land to potentially devour every creature in every body of water in the surrounding area.

❯ "Invasion of the Snakeheads," *Smithsonian,* smithsonianmag.com

That never came to pass, luckily, thanks to the crowds of brave citizens with pitchforks, along with the fish's extreme pyrophobia.

When hermit crabs detect the odor of a deceased member of their own kind, they do not become depressed, nor do they become consumed with existential dread. A more accurate description of their reaction would be "giddy." And that's because not only does the stench of death emanating from one of their fellows signal the possibility of acquiring a fancier shell than the one they're currently hauling around, but it also means an easy meal has just become available.

Sure it's repulsive to think about eating a dead homeowner and callously taking his place, but have you seen the rent nowadays for New York City apartments?

❯ "Cannibalistic Hermit Crabs Salivate at the Smell of Their Dead," *Smithsonian,* smithsonianmag.com

Mother Nature seems to have been determined to turn the small North American fish called the pirate perch (*Aphredoderus sayanus*) into a punch line. While she likely had little to do with the crudely sexual connotations inherent in its common name, or how portions of its scientific name are equally as suggestive, she was directly responsible for something even more embarrassing. As a pirate perch matures, its anus migrates gradually from the place you would assume an anus would belong, to directly underneath its throat.

> "Pirate Perch—
> *Aphredoderus sayanus*,"
> Ohio Department of
> Natural Resources,
> wildlife.ohiodnr.gov

If you happen to believe in ironic reincarnation, the existence of this fish alone should be enough to stop you from telling dirty jokes in mixed company ever again.

Even if you go as far as the North Pole to take a dip in the ocean, you're still not totally safe from the threat of a shark attack. Because the ancient and ghastly-looking Greenland shark (*Somniosus microcephalus*) calls those chilly waters home. And you shouldn't let the fact that they're nearly all blind (because of an eyeball-eating parasite, but more on that later) put your mind at ease, considering that these great white–sized leviathans have been witnessed eating polar bears and reindeer. They can also live for more than hundreds of years and are shunned by fishermen due to their having the most toxic flesh of any shark.

But if you do decide to brave the freezing waters, perhaps the extreme shrinkage will either make the sharks think you're just not worth their time or cause them to take pity on your misfortune.

> "Polar Bear Eaten by Shark: Who's Top Predator?" Reuters, reuters.com; "A 400-Year-Old Shark? Greenland Shark Could Be Earth's Longest-lived Vertebrate," *Los Angeles Times*, latimes.com

The family of reef-dwelling doofuses called boxfish (Ostraciidae) includes members that are among the stupidest-looking creatures in the sea. They can be very colorful, however, and that quality has made them fairly popular in the aquarium trade. But keeping a boxfish can be a rather tricky affair, especially if you expect it to coexist with other species of fish. Because when it feels threatened, it just might release a deadly chemical that kills every fish in the tank, including itself.

They're a great pet for history buffs, though. After all, since the fall of the Soviet Union, where else nowadays can you see the kind of "mutually assured destruction" scenario that was all the rage back in the 1950s?

> "Boxfish Tankmates," FishChannel.com, fishchannel.com

Anoplogastridae, the family of deep-water fish known as fangtooths (or ogrefish), won't impress you with their size, since they don't grow much longer than about 6 inches. But big (or at least disturbingly heinous) things can come in small packages, and these fish prove it with their disproportionately humongous teeth. The fangs on the lower jaws of these minuscule monstrosities are the largest of any fish, proportional to size. They're so preposterously long that fangtooths need special sockets on either side of their brains just so that they're able to close their mouths.

> "Fangtooth (*Anoplogaster cornuta*)," *Sea and Sky*, seasky.org

That might sound a bit grotesque, but it's really no different than the large cavity Jay Leno has presumably developed in his upper chest in order to accommodate his chin.

We don't normally associate octopuses with being deadly poisonous, but *Hapalochlaena* sure as hell are. That's the genus that includes all three (in addition to plenty more that have yet to be thoroughly described) known species of blue-ringed octopus, which lurks in the shallows from Japan to Australia. And every single one of them packs enough poison to kill a roomful of humans. What makes them so treacherous is the fact that they contain a substance in their saliva known as tetrodotoxin, which causes a paralysis that can make you appear clinically dead but fully aware (right up until the point when you're all the way dead, just a few minutes later). And the best part? They might not even have to bite you for the poison to enter your bloodstream.

So what does that mean exactly? Are Australians licking them like toads? Judging by some of the actors they've sent over here, it's not all that implausible.

> ❯ "Blue-Ringed Octopuses, *Hapalochlaena maculosa*," Marinebio, marinebio.org; "What Makes Blue-Rings So Deadly? Blue-Ringed Octopuses Have Tetrodotoxin," The Cephalopod Page, thecephalopodpage.org

For years mankind has marveled at the complexity and haunting qualities of whale "songs." The sonorous tones of the blue whale (*Balaenoptera musculus*), the largest of the mighty cetaceans, have long been studied by scientists. But recently researchers were forced to recalibrate their listening equipment after they noticed something strange: Whales' voices are getting deeper. And while theories abound, so far there's no solid explanation as to why. All they know for certain is that since as far back as the 1960s, in every area in which they live, blue whale tonal frequencies have been going down incrementally every single year.

> ❯ "Blue Whales Singing with Deeper Voices," Phys.org, phys.org

The explanation is probably very simple. And by "very simple," I mean, "Oh shit, the whales are getting seriously pissed."

There are a number of water-dwelling fiends that have been given the ominous designation of "tigerfish," but the worst of the lot is surely *Hydrocynus vittatus*. This African freshwater menace earned a measure of fame after Jeremy Wade, host of the show *River Monsters*, implicated the extraordinarily toothy species as the culprit responsible for a number of maulings in Botswana. But the locals knew all about the dangers of *Hydrocynus vittatus* well before Mr. Wade ever showed up, since tigerfish were already quite infamous for their appalling habit of jumping out of the water to snatch birds right out of the air.

> "This African Fish Can Catch and Eat Flying Birds," *Popular Science*, popsci.com

You have to admit, though, sneaking a few of these fish into a flamingo exhibit would be a hell of a lot more entertaining than any dolphin show.

You may not have been aware that limpets, those barnacle-looking sea snails that don't do much of anything besides stick to rocks all day, have teeth. And if that wasn't enough to furrow your brow, scientists have discovered that the choppers of the common limpet (*Patella vulgata*) are the strongest biological material known to man. You know how people always marvel at how strong spider silk is? Well, limpet teeth make that stuff look like tissue paper.

This information should in no way suggest or promote the viability of using spiderwebs as toilet paper. This practice is both ineffective and a source of great aggravation for the hatching spiderlings within the webs.

> "Extreme Strength Observed in Limpet Teeth," The Royal Society Publishing, rsif.royalsocietypublishing.org

There are a few undersea creatures that make their way through life in a noble manner, by providing a service to others. One such species is the bluestreak cleaner wrasse (*Labroides dimidiatus*), which is so named because they have a blue streak. Oh, and also because they're known for cleaning the gunk off of the skin of much larger fish. They'll even set up "stations," where customers looking to get their parasites and dead skin removed can stop by for an exfoliating session. Unfortunately, the wrasse have a sociopathic doppelgänger called *Aspidontus taeniatus*, or more commonly, the sabre-toothed blenny. While this surreptitious species mimics the wrasse to a tee, it does not share their zeal for philanthropy. The blenny will use its disguise to infiltrate one of the wrasse's cleaning stations, and approach one of the large fish that's expecting to get a little work done around the edges. And then the blenny will reward that fish's misplaced trust by biting a chunk out of its face. At which point the blenny will quickly hurry off and leave the wrasse to take the blame.

The message here is pretty clear: Trust no one, especially not a barber whose name comes anything even remotely close to "sabre-toothed."

> "Aspidontus taeniatus Quoy and Gaimard, 1834," Fishbase, fishbase.org

Brightly colored male guppies are as elegant in appearance as their scientific name is to the ear: *Poecilia reticulata*. And they're also so aggressively horny during mating season that the females (which are much drabber than their counterparts) have to remain constantly on the run from the males to avoid their potentially injurious advances. The females can become so desperate to escape the unwanted attention that they'll purposely place themselves within reach of their own predators, just to avoid being sexually assaulted.

So that explains why that girl I always talk to at Starbucks suddenly became a foster parent to seventeen Rottweilers.

> "Guppy Females Take Risks to Avoid Harassment," ScienceDaily, sciencedaily.com

The extreme deep-sea fish known as the stoplight loosejaw (*Malacosteus niger*) has an appearance that's even more absurd than its name. And "absurd," in this particular case, means "an abomination before God." But let's just focus on its face. In addition to dead eyes with red-and-green-light-emitting organs (hence the "stoplight" portion of its name) underneath to help it see in the dark, there's also the matter of its mouth, which is multi-hinged and can swing out in such a way that it looks like it's being decapitated (explaining the origin of the "loosejaw" part). That lower jaw is filled with needle-like teeth and oddly has no bottom floor of skin, so it's essentially used like one of those spike traps that were all the rage among the Vietcong back in the day.

❯ "Stoplight Loosejaw: *Idiacanthus antrostomus*," Oceana, oceana.org

Adding to that comparison, prolonged viewing of the stoplight loosejaw can also be useful for those wanting to experience the same type of Vietnam-style flashbacks that the homeless mumbling guy behind the bowling alley has.

Reproduction among brown trout (*Salmo trutta*) involves a lot of moving parts, both literally and figuratively. Everything has to fall into place with exact precision in order for the operation to be a success, even though there's no actual physical interaction between the males and females. The way it works is that the females have to lay their eggs on the ground, at roughly the same moment that the males release their sperm. Unfortunately this method leads to a lot of less-than-desirable suitors showing up to horn in on the action. So the females have learned a gambit straight out of *When Harry Met Sally*: faking their orgasms. Normally, the signal that trout females use to indicate they're ready for sex is to "[quiver] violently with their mouths open." But if the female thinks her partner is a little too lowbrow for her tastes, she'll violently quiver but neglect to drop any eggs, tricking the male into ejaculating pointlessly into the dirt.

❯ "Something Fishy about Trout Orgasm," *Telegraph*, telegraph.co.uk

It may seem a little mean, but at least the females aren't dissuading the males by laughing at the size of their penises. Which is downright cruel, and something for which I may never forgive my old high school girlfriend.

The ocean isn't the only place you can be terrified by stingrays. In fact, the biggest one around lives in freshwater in places like Indochina and Australia. And this creature can reportedly grow into a 1,300-pound, 16-foot pancake of terror. One reason to be afraid should a giant freshwater stingray (*Himantura polylepis*) decide to turn on you, aside from the whole venom thing, is that the 15-inch stilettos on the tips of their tails will surely kill you long before the poison does.

❯ *"Car-Size Stingray May Be World's Largest Freshwater Fish,"* National Geographic, nationalgeographic.com; "Giant Freshwater Stingray," Animal Planet, animalplanet.com

Remarkably, these giant rays weren't even described by science until 1990. Fishermen in Thailand have been describing them for centuries, however, mostly in the language of shrieks.

The cookiecutter shark (*Isistius brasiliensis*) sounds like it might be something cute, until the "shark" part sinks in. The reason they have that cutesy name is because of how they attack their prey. These miniature sharks sneak up and attach themselves to much larger animals, grab hold with their serrated teeth, twist out a cookie-shaped chunk of flesh, and then scram. For many years scientists were puzzled by the circular wounds (sometimes in the dozens) left on the carcasses of whales and other sea creatures that washed up on shore. Until they found it was just a total bastard of a shark.

❯ *"Cookiecutter Sharks, Isistius brasiliensis,"* Marinebio, marinebio.org

Which must have come as a big relief to the much maligned "melon baller squid," which was so named simply due to their love of the all-you-can-eat brunch at Golden Corral.

Cichlid fish of the genus *Nimbochromis* make their home in East Africa's Lake Malawi, and they're really good at "playing dead." However, the reason they do it isn't to trick predators into leaving them alone. The fact is, they're the predators. These cichlids will frequently flop onto their sides and sink to the bottom in the manner of a fishy corpse, and then when some unsuspecting scavenger (who thinks he might have just found a nice decomposing fish to nom on) shows up to investigate, the cichlid springs to life and eats it.

> ›*Cichlids: Understanding Angelfish, Oscars, Discus, and Others* by David Alderton

A technique that may also be useful at the beach, for those who don't mind the moral qualms involved in simulating a drowning victim in order to get to first base with a lifeguard.

Octopus tentacles can act autonomously even after being severed from the main body of the animal. They will wriggle and squirm for a disconcertingly long time, all by their lonesome, and this fun fact is the reason why about a half dozen people who enjoy eating raw octopus die every single year in South Korea, where the dish is served in restaurants.

> ›"Octopus Arms Found to Have 'Minds' of Their Own," *National Geographic*, nationalgeographic.com; "World's Most Dangerous Foods," *Travel + Leisure*, travelandleisure.com

They say this is because the tentacles are getting caught in people's throats, but we can't completely rule out the possibility that some of them are wrapping their suckers around kitchen knives and having protracted knife battles with the customers.

Octopuses of all sorts are perfectly capable of exiting the water and slurping along the ground for brief periods. When they're kept captive in a tank and there's food available in another part of the room, they've been known to open their enclosures and make their way across the floor to reach whatever it is they'd like to sink their beaks into. Then, after they're finished, they laboriously sucker and slop back whence they came. That is, if they don't decide to slither out or under the door and down a toilet.

> ›"Legging It: Evasive Octopus Who Has Been Allowed to Look for Love," *Independent*, independent.co.uk

I suppose this might explain the double mystery of my missing Doritos and the tentacle prints on my butt.

The echinoderms of the class Asteroidea that we refer to as starfish don't really have mouths to swallow things. But they have to get food inside their bellies somehow, so they've evolved to take the rather direct approach of spewing one of their sticky, acidic stomachs out of their bodies and onto prey (or into prey, should it be a shellfish). Once their victim is sufficiently enveloped, the starfish then digests it alive over the course of hours, and sometimes days. And if a starfish accidentally attacks something with an above-average ability to defend itself, and it results in one or more of its arms getting torn off, that's no big deal at all. They'll just grow a new one in no time flat.

These abilities sure would come in handy at one of those Las Vegas buffets after a long day of counting cards at the blackjack table. And when they drag you to the back and start in with the pliers, the joke will be on them when your thumbs grow right back the very next day!

> "Sea Star," Science Learning Hub, sciencelearn.org.nz

The giant hagfish (*Eptatretus goliath*) is an evolutionarily ancient creature, and is the only one known (not involved in federal-level politics) that has a squishy, cartilaginous skull but no spine. The way they protect themselves from predators is by excreting copious amounts of slime. But it's no ordinary slime—this stuff is powerful enough to gag a shark and can gum up the gills of an offending fish so much that it can cause the fish to drown. And just in case you were getting any bright ideas about acquiring an exotic new pet, be aware that leaving a hagfish in an aquarium will soon result in a tank that's completely filled with sticky goop.

> "Scientists Film Hagfish Anti-Shark Slime Weapon," Phys.org, phys.org

You know, pretty much like the average teenager's sock drawer.

Relative to body size, barnacles have the world's longest penises and can stretch them out until they're ten times as long as themselves. This little factoid may not be alarming in and of itself (unless you're a female barnacle), but there's more to it than that. They can also control the size and shape of said appendage like a girthy accordion, and scientists have even found that barnacles can grow new penises every year (they tend to snap off in rough seas) in a way that's specific to the environment they currently occupy. For instance, barnacles that are spaced far apart will grow stretchier penises, those that are exposed to constant waves will be wider for extra durability, and so on.

❯"To Find Love, the Barnacle Grows a Stretchy, Accordion-Like Penis," *Discover*, discovermagazine.com

Something like that would definitely come in handy when you need to use the bathroom but don't want to leave your seat in the movie theater. And also for defending yourself when the management attempts to have you removed.

The pistol shrimp (family Alpheidae) comes equipped with a modified, oversized claw that isn't just for show. It can clamp shut with such velocity that the resulting shockwave can raise the surrounding water temperature to 7,000 degrees Fahrenheit and actually kill nearby fish. Thankfully they're rather small, but that doesn't stop them from being a major source of underwater noise pollution, to where their incessant snapping interferes with sonar communications.

❯"Incredible Slo-Mo Footage of the Pistol Shrimp's Devastating Attack," Gizmodo, gizmodo.com

Now if we can just get these crafty crustaceans to do our bidding, we'd have an ingenious way of sending enemy submarines into the rocks with perfectly plausible deniability. Hey, stop staring. It certainly wouldn't be the stupidest plan the military has ever come up with.

"Penis fencing" isn't just an activity for high school locker rooms and/or federal penitentiaries. Those words also accurately describe the mating behavior of many types of flatworms. Species like . . . I swear to God this is its name . . . *Pseudobiceros hancockanus* have evolved phalluses that are hard and sharp, and the worms can wield them both offensively and defensively. And since these animals are hermaphrodites, the actual sex basically involves two lower life forms stabbing the crap out of one another.

> "World's Weirdest: Flatworm Penis Fencing," *National Geographic*, nationalgeographic.com

Which doesn't sound altogether different from what I imagine at least a few of Billy Bob Thornton's six marriages were like.

The fish in the family Triglidae are called "gurnards," which is supposed to be an approximation of the grunting croaks they make when removed from the water by disappointed fishermen. They're also referred to as sea robins, by people who apparently have never seen a bird before in their lives. Different species range from looking like mutated frogs with wings to huge armored insects (neither of which keeps seafood enthusiasts from finding them delicious), but the one thing all of them have in common is the pectoral fins on either side of their bodies, which have evolved into six spidery "legs." These spiny appendages allow them to stir up the dirt for scraps and scuttle along the ocean floor in a very un-fishlike manner, thereby accomplishing the nearly impossible task of making them even more abominable.

> "*Aspitrigla cuculus* (Linnaeus, 1758)," Habitas, habitas.org.uk

Remember that scene in the 1982 remake of The Thing, *where the guy's severed head sprouts legs and somebody says, "You gotta be f***ing kidding"? It's pretty much like that, but much better when coated with flour and fried in olive oil.*

Tangs, a family of fish (Acanthuridae) that includes Dory from *Finding Nemo*, are also known as surgeonfish because of the scalpel-like blades on either side of their tails. They have the ability (which we can only hope gets some screen time in one of the sequels) to whip these improvised switchblades out at a moment's notice and shank you like a convict in the prison yard.

> ＞*All Stings Considered: First Aid and Medical Treatment of Hawaii's Marine Injuries* by Craig Thomas, MD, and Susan Scott

So that's why she's always so "forgetful." She's clearly playing dumb to avoid being implicated in any number of ongoing murder investigations.

Sport fishing is a lot of fun. At least until the thing at the end of your line skewers you like a cocktail olive. For example, in 2015 there was a man-killed-by-angry-swordfish incident in which a charter boat captain in Hawaii shot a spear gun into a 6-foot specimen. In response, the swordfish launched itself at the captain and successfully lodged its spear into his upper chest.

The fish then presumably exclaimed, "I think he got the point!" and, when nobody laughed, sighed and swam away in a huff.

＞"Swordfish Kills Fisherman Who Was Trying to Catch It in Hawaii," CNN, cnn.com

A stingray in Florida launched itself out of the water and onto a boat where it killed a fisherman by stabbing him in the heart. And if you're grumbling right now about the extra expense of having to buy a bulletproof vest just to go fishing, you needn't bother with all of that. Because two years later another ray hurled itself onto another boat, and killed a woman purely with the force of the impact.

> ＞"Stingray Leaps into Boat, Stings Florida Man in Heart," *National Geographic*, nationalgeographic.com; "Woman Killed as Stingray Leaps into Boat in U.S.," *Telegraph*, telegraph.co.uk

So far, the best precaution you can take with regard to fishing in Florida is to buy a motorhome and drive to Wisconsin.

***Moby-Dick* tells the fantastic tale of a one-legged man's quest for vengeance** against a particularly dickish sperm whale. But the story may not be all that fantastic after all, considering the antisocial antagonist was based on a real-life albino whale with an even more potentially offensive-sounding name: Mocha Dick. The nonfiction version gained much renown in the days of yore for being much larger than the average whale, as well as for sinking ships out of pure spite. Also, Mocha Dick is said to have had multiple harpoons sticking out of its back— the result of many failed attempts to bring the grumpy leviathan to heel.

❯"Was There a Real Moby Dick?" New Bedford Whaling Museum, whalingmuseum.org

So, if the purchase of a DVD that includes the words Mocha Dick in the title happens to show up on your credit card statement, just tell your wife that you're a big fan of whaling history.

Every year a place called Christmas Island (off the coast of Australia) is overrun with red crabs (*Gecarcoidea natalis*). They don't just scuttle onto the beach, drop a few eggs, and call it a day. When mating season rolls around, 40–50 million of these carnally motivated crustaceans will advance steadily inland, shutting down traffic and causing residents to shelter in their homes. Sustaining themselves partially on human trash, they'll spend the next few weeks having terrifying crab sex and then finally return to shore to spew their eggs into the sea.

❯"Red Crab Migration," Christmas Island Tourism Association, christmas.net.au

So if you're planning a vacation to Christmas Island and notice the rates are inexplicably cheap during one particular part of the year, now you'll know what's up. Don't be a sucker.

CHAPTER 2

Backstabbing Birds and Other Airborne Atrocities

Bats are obviously horrid creatures, but because birds tend to be pleasing to the eye they seem to pass under the radar when really they're just as creepy or even more so. Birds are nothing but smaller, sneakier versions of dinosaurs, and we must never forget that. The ancient fiery cataclysm that brought about their forebears' demise should have forced a little humility on their squawking kind, but that doesn't appear to be the case, judging from the preponderance of cocky pigeons and uppity blue jays. Perhaps there aren't many birds that can take a human's life (directly at least), but there are certainly a few with the capability. But should we ever let down our guard around even the lowliest of sparrows, who's to say that they won't one day choose to regain the lost glory of their ancestors in a frenzy of violent, chirpy revolution? And if that day should come, we can expect the remainder of our existence to be unpleasant indeed and filled with alternating moments of terror and disgust, as we are forced to witness behavior such as . . .

Northern fulmar (old Norse for "foul gull") chicks protect themselves from danger by puking a glue-like secretion. Not only is the substance acidic, atrocious-smelling, and nearly impossible to remove, but the projectile vomit also can cause an attacking bird's feathers to mat up so that it can no longer fly properly. The chemicals in the oily discharge also eat away at the waterproof coating so that the next time the bird lands on the water it will drown.

❯ "Northern Fulmar: *Fulmarus glacialis*," The Alfred Denny Museum of Zoology, admuseumguide.weebly.com

Apparently "just let it roll off your back" isn't such great advice when you're talking about alien barf.

Taking a slightly different but equally offensive approach, the chicks of the Eurasian roller (*Coracias garrulus*) vomit noxious orange fluid all over themselves when in danger. And when their parents are away, the repugnant smell of the chicks' upchuck alerts them that something is amiss back at the nest. As far as scientists know, this form of communicating via puke is unique to birds. Hopefully.

If we could come up with a similar system for parents of college-age kids, we could make a fortune. We'd call it the "Fast Response and Alerts to Tequila Sickness" device, or "FRATS" for short.

❯ "'Vomit Bird' Throws Up a Defense Against Predators," Seeker, seeker.com

It seems rather odd that the roadrunner (*Geo-coccyx californianus*) is painted as the victim in those old Warner Bros. cartoons, seeing as how in reality they're just as bloodthirsty as coyotes. Moreover, the blood they crave comes from a rather terrifying source: rattle-snakes. They'll also happily gobble down tarantula hawks (a horrifically monstrous wasp) and other species of birds. The way the roadrunner ends its prey's life is by repeatedly slamming the victim's face into the dirt and pecking out its eyes. Then, depending on how big the victim is, the road-runner will either swallow it all at once or let one portion dangle out of its mouth while the rest gets digested.

With that in mind, maybe Jigsaw's big catchphrase in the Saw *movies shouldn't have been "I want to play a game" but "Meep meep."*

❯ "Greater Roadrunner," The Wild Bird Store, wildbirdsonline.com; "Greater Roadrunner," The Cornell Lab of Ornithology, allaboutbirds.org

Bringing home a cockatiel or a parakeet from the pet store can sometimes result in more than simply turning your home into an annoying, stinking screech-fest. That is, if it happens to be a carrier of something called "parrot fever." And parrots aren't the only birds that can infect you with the rare affliction known as *psittacosis* (which is a potentially life-threatening form of chlamydia). So, just to be safe, you might also want to avoid pigeons, doves, mynah birds, and turkeys. Oh, and also sheep, goats, and cows.

❯ "Compendium of Measures to Control *Chlamydia psittaci* Infection among Humans (Psittacosis) and Pet Birds (Avian Chlamydiosis), 1998," Centers for Disease Control and Prevention, cdc.gov; "Psittacosis," New York State Department of Health, health.ny.gov

Um, if this is anywhere close to the same chlamydia I learned about in school, apparently there are a lot of animals that are just as "open-minded" about sex as your parents were in the 1970s.

The shrike is a cute little bird that commits grisly murder in a way that would make Vlad the Impaler proud. There are thirty diabolical species of them, with the largest genus being *Lanius*. That's Latin for "butcher," and should give you a pretty significant clue as to what's coming next. After catching a mouse, lizard, or even another bird, the shrike's preferred method of ending its victims' lives is by hauling them up to a thorny branch, cactus, or even a barbed-wire fence and then skewering them on something pointy until the wriggling stops.

Just for fun, try letting one of these loose at a PetSmart. Then come back the next morning and offer your services as a gerbil exorcist.

❯ "The Strange World of the Shrike," National Wildlife Federation, nwf.org

As creepy as they are, there's no real reason to lose sleep fretting about any of the three species of vampire bats flying around. What you should be worried about is them *running* around. While most bats are about as agile as a spastic trout when forced to land on the ground, vampire bats can not only walk but run. In fact, their gait is better described as a gallop, and resembles what a fast-moving gorilla would look like if it had leathery wings and drank blood. It makes sense when you consider the ways these bats feed, which is by sneaking up on large mammals in the dead of night, and then stealthily crawling up their legs.

❯ "Unlike Other Bats, Vampire Bats Keep Out of Trouble by Running, Cornell Researchers Find," *Cornell Chronicle*, news.cornell.edu

After all, if you were the size of a mouse and had to maneuver around the hooves of massive beasts that could easily stomp you into putty, you'd learn to haul ass too.

Perhaps there actually is a legitimate reason to be afraid of bats on the leathery wing—at least if you live in Peru. Over the past several years there have been some alarming reports of a surge in attacks on humans there. In fact, government health workers in 2010 were forced to respond to jungle-adjacent communities with emergency rabies vaccinations when more than 500 people were bitten in a remarkably short period of time.

It was the only course of action left, since the Peruvian president was apparently too proud to take the much cheaper option of hiring Wesley Snipes to deal with the problem.

> ❯"Rabid Bats Attack over 500 Indians in Peru Jungle," Reuters, reuters.com

Parrots for the most part are beautiful birds, and entertaining enough to be

a favored pet among the elderly and eccentric weirdoes alike. But watching them have sex can be a trying ordeal, especially where white-fronted parrots (*Amazona albifrons*), a species native to Central America, are concerned. This is mainly because this particular bird's idea of courtship is for the males to vomit directly into the females' mouths. And while that may be par for the course in terms of how many birds feed their young, it's an activity that has no place in the bedroom.

> ❯"Want Some Vomit with That Kiss?" The Earth Story, the-earth-story.com

Unless, of course, both parties are so repulsive that large amounts of tequila are required to get the job done, and a little regurgitation is simply an acceptable risk.

It appears that Donald Duck's frequent psychotic episodes and propensity for fits of uncontrollable rage may have some basis in reality. Male ducks of various species are known to team up to sexually assault females, sometimes to the point of accidentally murdering the object of their desire. Some females have actually evolved specialized "convoluted" vaginas to thwart the hostile entry of the males' corkscrew-shaped penises. And sometimes a male duck's frenzied, deviant urges will even lead it to engage in acts of homosexual necrophilia.

If you think the Washington Redskins are having problems with their name, wait until people start accusing the Anaheim Ducks of being insensitive to the victims of gay necrophiliac gang rapists.

❯"Necrophilia among Ducks Ruffles Research Feathers," *Guardian*, theguardian.com; "Ballistic Penises and Corkscrew Vaginas—the Sexual Battles of Ducks," *National Geographic*, phenomena.nationalgeographic.com

And while there are a number of ducks with a tendency toward the old ultra-violence, the most antisocial of them all might be the flying steamer duck (*Tachyeres patachonicus*) of South America. The surliest of the four species of steamer ducks, it's also the only one that can fly. And it further overcompensates for its shortcomings with a willingness to fight anyone and anything at a moment's notice like a roid-raging drunk at a fraternity bar. Their notoriously bad attitude manifests itself especially during mating season, when the steamer ducks will use the specialized pummeling knobs on their wings to pulverize any waterfowl in the vicinity, often to death.

❯"Attack of the Flying Steamer Ducks," ScienceBlogs, scienceblogs.com

They can easily be distinguished from other species by their peculiar mating call, which sounds eerily like, "Come at me, bro! Come at me, bro!"

Ducklings, indisputably some of the cutest things that have ever existed in the galaxy, will occasionally cannibalize one another. And when they do, it's not because they're starving after an especially harsh winter or anything like that. No, researchers believe that the reason baby ducks sometime engage in fratricide and then gobble one another up like downy, squeaking hors d'oeuvres is because . . . they're bored.

❯ "Brooding and Rearing Ducks," NSW Government, dpi.nsw. gov.au

Which could be a highly effective argument for children when trying to convince their parents to reconsider their initial refusal to buy them both a drum kit and a pony for Christmas.

Certain varieties of parrots are pretty good at imitating sounds (and loudly repeating profanities), but they're rank amateurs compared to the world champion of avian mimicry: the lyrebirds of Australia. There are two species in the lyrebird genus, including a "superb" one (*Menura novaehollandiae*) and the "Albert's" (*Menura alberti*), which has the misfortune of being named after the Prince Albert of penis-piercing fame. Both of these birds can perfectly replicate not just the sound of the human voice but also other noises like car alarms, chainsaws, and even a blaster from *Star Wars*.

And if you think all that sounds just fantastic, then you clearly never had one living in your neighbor's backyard.

❯ "Lyrebird Perfectly Imitates Laser Gun Sounds," ScienceAlert, sciencealert.com

There are a lot of animals in the world with the word *vampire* attached to their names, and some that probably don't really deserve such a dire designation. However, in the case of the nasty little bird from the Galápagos called *Geospiza difficilis septentrionalis*, it's entirely justified. Since the volcanic island on which the vampire finch lives is subject to frequent drought, it has learned to put the sharp beak its ancestors employed for eating seeds to quite a different purpose: pecking holes in other birds and lapping up their dripping blood. Their preferred victim is a group of birds called boobies, and the finches are sure to avoid inflicting permanent harm on said boobies so that they can return again and again to abuse them.

Also, vampire finches are part of the group of birds Charles Darwin used as evidence for his theory in his most important work, "Attack of the Boobiesuckers." Or maybe that was just something I saw on Cinemax.

> "Vampire Finches a.k.a. Sharp-Beaked Finches, Sharp-Billed Ground Finches," Beauty of Birds, beautyofbirds.com

Hood mockingbirds (*Mimus macdonaldi*) are very inquisitive and have little fear of humans. You will surely delight in the company of such gregarious creatures, right up until they start pecking your legs into hamburger. These birds come from the Galápagos Islands, which is a place where it can be tough to find a drink. And the hood mockingbirds have become either so brazen or so desperate that they'll readily approach you like they want to be your pal, and then start ripping away at any scabs on your legs to feast on the juiciness within.

> "Hood Mockingbird (*Mimus macdonaldi*)," Wildscreen Arkive, arkive.org

This is just another reason why if you mention the Galápagos Islands to a birdwatcher, he'll often just stare off into the distance, mumble quietly to himself, and begin to weep.

As if vultures weren't repugnant enough already, there are some that up the ante considerably in the way they keeps themselves cool on a hot summer day—by unloading their bowels all over themselves. Since New World vultures like turkey vultures (*Cathartes aura*) don't sweat, the way they regulate their temperature is by defecating and urinating freely all over their own legs. Certain storks do the same thing, but vultures get a side benefit. Since buzzard crap is so vile that even bacteria can't stand it, it actually helps keep their legs free from infection.

———

So when you're injured out in the middle of nowhere and vultures start closing in, try not to panic. If you play your cards right, maybe they'll just shit on you and save your life. And then eat you.

❯"Fun Facts about Turkey Vultures," Wild Birds Unlimited, wbu.com; "Rule #60: Figure Out What Kind of Vulture is Circling You," Audubon, Audubon.org

Pelicans of all varieties eat a wide range of fish.

We expect that much out of those goofy-looking weirdoes. What's a bit more shocking is when they gulp down their fellow birds. From snarfing down pigeons in a public park to gobbling the occasional baby penguin, pelicans have no reservations about murdering just about anything that will fit into their fat, greedy mouths.

In other news, Taylor Swift, Russell Crowe, and Robin Thicke have all been rumored to be increasing security at their beach homes.

❯"Pelican's Pigeon Meal Not So Rare," BBC News, bbc.co.uk

New Zealand is where you can find the world's only alpine parrot, the kea (*Nestor notabilis*). They're rather drab for a parrot but are nonetheless notable for their extremely high intelligence and strange habit of tearing the rubber linings from car windows. And also for eating sheep alive. Ranchers nearly drove the kea to extinction due to its rather un-parroty habit of landing on the backs of livestock, using its curved beak to part the wool, and then carving out the fat from underneath the skin.

While this behavior probably wouldn't kill a sheep directly, the ranchers knew they would have trouble selling their wares to the Yarn Barn with everything covered in putrefied gore.

> "On the Habits of the Kea, the Sheep-Eating Parrot of New Zealand," *Nature*, nature.com

The "sacs" on the unfortunately named greater sac-winged bats (*Saccopteryx bilineata*) serve a purpose that's disgusting even for bats. The males fill said sacs with urine, which they collect and transfer using their mouths, along with some other penile secretions they coax forth by rubbing their necks against their groins. Once their little bags of horrible tricks are filled to satisfaction, they waft the foul odor of this odious concoction toward nearby females, who consider this act to be irresistibly seductive.

> "The Bats That Mix Nature's Grossest Perfume," BBC, bbc.com

This seemingly repulsive approach obviously has a proven track record, because if it didn't then Old Spice would have gone out of business years ago.

It's easy to forget sometimes that birds evolved from dinosaurs, but not when you're in the presence of the hoatzin (*Opisthocomus hoazin*). Also commonly known as the stinkbird, these bizarre-looking Amazonian swamp squawkers are a bit of a mystery to scientists. Not because they stink, which they most definitely do, but because their chicks are the only birds on the planet with working claws.

❯ "Hoatzin: Meet the Stink Bird," Discover Wildlife, discoverwildlife.com

We don't know a whole lot about these birds, possibly because there's just so much weirdness going on that researchers are proceeding with extra caution. After all, nobody wants to end up like the tubby guy from Jurassic Park, with a face full of poison vomit.

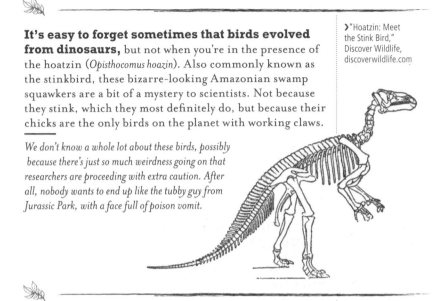

There are twenty species of bowerbirds in the family Ptilonorhynchidae, and what's particularly notable about all of them is their unusual mating behavior. The way bowerbirds attract the ladies is by building elaborate nests, which they decorate with sticks and shiny doodads for extra effect. And scientists recently found that the males often build these structures in such a way that they trick the females, by way of optical illusions like forced perspective, into thinking that they're much bigger than they actually are.

❯ "Bowerbirds Trick Mates with Optical Illusions," *Nature*, nature.com

They use the power of crappy magic to trick women into having sex? So why aren't they called the "David Blaine bird"?

Anoura fistulata, otherwise known as the Ecuadorian tube-lipped nectar bat, has a disturbing physical feature that's above and beyond the normal bat-related ickiness. In order to extricate the sugary goodness from within the extraordinarily deep flowers that are its primary food source, it has evolved a snaking tongue that's 150 percent as long as its body.

Apparently it can also hover, so I guess rabies can now be moved off of the list of top bat-related fears and replaced with "wet willies."

❯ "The Bat with the Incredibly Long Tongue," *New Scientist*, newscientist.com

Golden eagles have a clever (and horrendous) way of dealing with hard-to-eat prey like turtles. These huge birds will grab the reptiles, fly way up high in the air, and then drop the poor things onto some rocks to crack open their shells. It's a tactic that has proven so successful that they've expanded it to include baby goats.

Sure, it sounds cruel, but unless you're the type of person who prepares lobster dinners by offering them a tiny pistol and the chance to say a few last words, you really don't have any right to judge.

❯ "Golden Eagle Droppings," Boston University, bu.edu

The ancient Greek playwright Aeschylus is believed to have been killed by an eagle. Which sounds pretty badass until you find out that the creature that was more directly responsible for his death was the turtle that the eagle dropped onto his head. Oddly enough, the playwright had been spending a lot of time outdoors, specifically because of a prophecy that foretold he would be killed by a falling object.

But what's really ironic is that Aeschylus is famous for writing tragedies. Because dying like that is pretty goddamn hilarious.

❯ "Aeschylus," Encyclopedia.com, encyclopedia.com

One doesn't normally associate ducks with horrifying teeth, but a few sure as hell have them. In fact, there's a whole genus of diving sea ducks called saw-bills (*Mergus*), and every member species is equipped with a serrated bill that's long and thin like a drywall saw. While they're not teeth exactly, they certainly do the job of shredding fish as well as any shark.

So now if you ever see an elderly man sitting on a park bench torn to pieces with a loaf of bloody, half-eaten bread in his hand, you'll know exactly what happened.

> "A Duck with Teeth in Raritan Bay," *Middletown Patch*, patch.com

Species of penguins like the Adélie penguin (*Pygoscelis adeliae*) have very sharp-edged bills, which is to be expected from a bird that hunts fish for a living. But they also have an array of sharp, backward-facing spines on both their tongues and their throats. These protrusions assist the penguins in assuring the demise of any creature foolish enough to think there might be even a remote possibility of squirming its way out of their mouths.

> "Diet and Feeding: Answers," Penguin Science, penguinscience.com

Thus explaining why when March of the Penguins *was released in the Antarctic, Morgan Freeman's voice was replaced by James Earl Jones in full Darth Vader mode.*

Speaking of Adélie penguins, not only are they orally reprehensible, but it turns out they're morally reprehensible as well. A 1998 study found that the females will prostitute themselves for rocks. Since building materials are often in short supply, these waddling delinquents will happily trade sex to get them. Which is especially egregious when you consider that this is a bird that forms lifelong mating pairs. And even worse, the females will sometimes rip off a sex-starved male by distracting him with a mating dance and then running off with his rock, presumably while he is busy fumbling in his wallet for one-dollar bills.

Researchers were also shocked to find that these transactions were all coordinated by specially evolved males that were easily recognizable due to their jewel-encrusted canes and large, purple-feathered hats.

❯ "Pick Up a Penguin," BBC News, bbc.co.uk; "Some Female Animals Don't Hesitate to Trade Their Bodies in Exchange for Material Gain," National Wildlife Federation, nwf.org

Thousands of penguins congregate in small areas every breeding season to lay their eggs and raise their chicks. There are all sorts of difficult obstacles they must overcome in order to ensure their reproduction efforts are a success—including what to do with their poop. Since filling up your home with your own crap is generally considered an unsound parenting practice, some penguin species, like the chinstrap (*Pygoscelis antarctica*) and Adélie, have modified their gastrointestinal systems to allow them to launch their feces in arcing trajectories well away from their nests.

❯ "Projectile Penguin Poop Pressures," ScienceBlogs, scienceblogs.com

The penguins, seals, and nature photographers who find themselves on the receiving end of a barrage of projectile penguin diarrhea probably don't appreciate this very much. But hey, survival of the fittest, right?

The gargantuan toilet accumulations created by penguins can build up to the point that the stain they make is actually visible via satellite imagery (and not the spy ones that can zoom in on your face). Researchers discovered this unsavory fact in 2009, when a mysterious brown blot on the landscape turned out to be a colony of emperor penguins (*Aptenodytes forsteri*). And now, when they want to know where penguins are hiding, that's become the standard way of finding them.

> ❯ "Penguin Poop Seen from Space," *National Geographic*, nationalgeographic.com

Sure, it's nauseating, but following a trail of filth probably isn't altogether different from the way Hollywood keeps tabs on Russell Brand.

Crows are really smart. Unnervingly so. Not only are their puzzle-solving abilities on par with a five-year-old human child, but they also have an uncanny ability to remember faces. Researchers have even discovered (after an unfortunate mass dive-bombing incident) that if you should ever wrong a crow, it will hold a grudge for years and form a posse to exact revenge.

But the important question here is, "How do you apologize?" Because I can't get a damn thing done with a thousand crows cawing outside my window. And it's not like I should be held responsible for what my cat did, anyway.

❯ "Hitchcockian Crows Spread the Word about Unkind Humans," Live Science, livescience.com

About a decade ago scientists in Germany and Sweden were baffled by a new phenomenon that was as perplexing as it was grotesque: exploding toads. Reports were coming in at an alarming rate of unfortunate amphibians that had apparently popped into a shower of entrails, for no apparent reason whatsoever. Finally, a culprit emerged, and it was crows. The birds had learned to sneak up and peck, with surgical precision, at the exact spot on the back of a toad where they could quickly extract its liver and then fly away unnoticed. Once the toad realized (far too late) that it had been assaulted, it would puff up in the way toads do as a defense mechanism, thereby sending its guts spewing out of the hole left by the crow.

❯ "Hungry Crows May Be Behind Exploding Toads," NBC News, nbcnews.com

Rumor has it that George R.R. Martin wrote an entire novel starring that three-eyed crow from Game of Thrones, *but HBO passed on turning it into a spinoff on the basis that it was "too violent and cruel."*

There's a bat in Madagascar that has suckers for feet. No joke. It's called the sucker-footed bat (*Myzopoda aurita*), possibly because calling it the "toilet-plunging ratbird" would have made it hard to raise money for any conservation efforts in the area. Their feet don't really use suction, however. The way they stick to things is by "wet adhesion," meaning their feet are sticky with some kind of nauseating bat fluid.

❯ "Pads Attach to Smooth Surfaces: Madagascar Sucker-Footed Bat," Ask Nature, asknature. org; "Sucker-Footed Bat Hangs Upright Via Sweat, Not Suction," *National Geographic*, nationalgeographic.com

The substance that makes the suckers work is actually called "modified sweat," which I can only hope doesn't mean it's derived entirely from their balls.

"Obligate siblicide" doesn't sound like a very nice practice, and it very much isn't. In birds, it means that one chick kills one or more of the other chicks in the nest. And worst of all, it's by design. A few birds, like the Verreaux's eagle (*Aquila verreauxii*), lay just two eggs, with the second serving only as insurance in case the first one doesn't make it. If the firstborn chick comes out healthy, however, it's curtains for the latecomer, as it is invariably pecked and bullied to death by its older brother or sister.

If only Martin Sheen had followed this protocol, America's long nightmare with Charlie could have been avoided.

❯"The Verreaux's Eagle—an Interview with Dr. Rob Davies," African Raptors, africanraptors.org

The cute little European songbirds known as chickadees (*Parus major*), also known as "great tits" (stop it), have developed a new feeding behavior: They're killing bats while they sleep. It was discovered in 2009 that bats hibernating in a Hungarian cave were being systematically decimated by flocks of ravenous tits. Taking advantage of their lethargic state, the perky little tits were swooping into the cave and feasting on the poor bats as they hung from their roosts, and sometimes carrying them, kicking and squeaking, back to their nests to murder them in broad daylight.

❯"Great Tits Acquire Taste for Bats," BBC News, bbc.co.uk

Just for your edification, other species of this bird include "stripe-breasted tits," "dusky tits," and "elegant tits." You're welcome.

The Eurasian blue tit (*Cyanistes caeruleus*) may be the cleverest of all the tits. And not in a good way. In England, these birds are renowned for their ability to ruin a decent breakfast, by unscrewing the caps from milk bottles and stealing the contents. For this crime, the public has assigned the blue tit another informal designation: the "cream thief."

> "Mystery Bird: Blue Tit, *Cyanistes caeruleus*," *Guardian*, theguardian. com

The British tabloids presumably covered this story for weeks, because nothing excites the reading public like creamy tits.

Not that there's anything wrong with it, but a certain percentage of all predatory birds are transvestites. Only they're not engaging in this behavior due to some internal gender-related conflict, but rather to trick females into having sex with them. Both the raptorial marsh harrier (*Circus aeruginosus*) and the marsh wading ruff (*Philomachus pugnax*) occasionally produce males that develop female plumage. They will retain this feminine look for the entirety of their lives, as it allows them a measure of protection from the more aggressive alpha males. It also lets them sneak under the radar and engage in a little hanky panky with the females when the more macho males aren't looking.

And my parents said I was crazy when I told them I wanted to spend the rest of my life as a Barbra Streisand impersonator and date supermodels.

> "Why Some Birds of Prey Become Transvestites," Live Science, livescience.com

The Canada goose population used to be in sharp decline, but conservation efforts were able to pull them back from the brink. It is a true success story in the annals of wildlife management. But on the flip side, they've since become so plentiful that it's getting ridiculous, and they're ruining parks and lakes with their incessant honking, aggressive demeanor, and nonstop bombardment of feces.

❯ "Canada Geese Damage Management: Public Health Issues," The Internet Center for Wildlife Damage Management, icwdm.org

But at least now that parks are turning into giant outdoor Slip 'N Slides, we now have an affordable alternative to taking the kids to those expensive bouncy houses.

Vultures are already pretty hardcore, but the species known as the bearded vulture (*Gypaetus barbatus*) is such a badass that the majority of its diet is bones. Or maybe it's just non-confrontational and doesn't mind eating last. At any rate, bearded vultures wait until after all the lions, hyenas, jackals, and other vultures have had their way with a carcass, and then glide in for the bony leftovers. To get at the marrow inside they'll crack the smaller ones open with their powerful beaks. And to get at the goopy deliciousness inside the bigger bones, bearded vultures will carry a femur or a spine high up into the sky and then drop it onto rocks.

❯ "The Bone Eating Bird," Reed College, reed.edu

Honestly, is there any more appropriate way for Ozzy Osbourne to finally meet his maker than to have his head caved in by a giant thighbone dropped by a vulture? Well, maybe cirrhosis.

The giant golden-crowned flying fox (*Acerodon jubatus*) has a regal name befitting its lofty position as the world's most humongous, creepy-ass bat. This species has a wingspan of 5 feet, which is roughly the size of Woody Allen, and its face really does look like it belongs on a fox. To enable it to silently swoop close enough to give you a heart attack, it incredibly weighs only around 2½ pounds.

> "Giant Golden-Crowned Flying-Fox," BatWorlds, batworlds.com

———

Which further reinforces the "a lot of creepy in a small package" Woody Allen comparison.

The African bird known as the drongo can perfectly mimic other species of birds, including a type of "sentry" bird that meerkats rely on to warn them when danger is near. Of course, drongos couldn't care less about meerkat safety—they just do it to trick the meerkats into leaving half-eaten food behind after scrambling down a hole. Meerkats aren't dumb, however, and won't fall for this ruse for long. So the drongos just switch things up, and imitate the terrified screech of an entirely different type of bird.

> "African Bird Shouts False Alarms to Deceive and Steal, Study Shows," *National Geographic*, nationalgeogrpahic.com

———

At which point the meerkats presumably start scratching out large letters in the dirt reading, "Hey eagles, some guy down here named 'Drongo' just said you're all a bunch of assholes."

The Bassian thrush (*Zoothera lunulata*) from southeastern Australia and Tasmania doesn't demean itself by scratching around in the dirt for bugs like a peasant. It takes the much classier approach of bending over and farting on the ground. That's not a lie. In order to dislodge insects from their hiding places, this bird will literally squat down, take aim at some leaf litter, and let loose with a blast of air from its ass.

Whereupon the bugs, rightly mortified at such undignified behavior, immediately express their displeasure in a strongly written letter to the minister of the interior. At which point the thrush stabs them in the face.

❯*Top 100 Birding Sites of the World* by Dominic Couzens

The bird with the longest beak on the planet isn't a stork or some ridiculous toucan—it's a cute little hummingbird. The sword-billed hummingbird (*Ensifera ensifera*—that's Latin for "sword-wielder," twice for emphasis) from the South American Andes essentially has an ice pick at the end of its face, and is the only bird with a beak that's longer than its body. It's so long that the bird has to hold it straight up in the air to avoid toppling over when perched. These hummingbirds probably use this adaptation for getting at hard-to-reach flowers or something delightful like that, and probably not for dealing harshly with any stool pigeons in their territory.

❯"Sword-Billed Hummingbirds," Beauty of Birds, beautyofbirds.com

Just saying, I certainly wouldn't recommend pissing one off, unless you're in the market for an iridescently whimsical lobotomy.

All six species of pitohui, a genus native to New Guinea, have a pretty unusual quality as far as birds are concerned: They're poisonous. However, we didn't have the slightest idea that they were toxic at all until 1989, when a researcher touched one, put his fingers in his mouth, and noticed his tongue had gone numb (science!). It's believed that these birds don't actually produce poison themselves, but eat vast quantities of a certain type of noxious beetle until they themselves are infused with batrachotoxin, which just so happens to be the same stuff that certain species of poison frogs use to ensure they get left the hell alone.

It's likely no coincidence that the name pitohui is so similar to the sound resulting from the average spit-take.

❯ "Hooded Pitohui," Aquarium of the Pacific, aquariumofpacific.org; "Birds of a (Toxic) Feather," *BioScience*, bioscience.oxfordjournals.org

Black herons (*Egretta ardesiaca*) have a dastardly way of tricking fish into becoming lunch. By drawing their wings above their head to form a "canopy" of sorts, they're able to plunge a circular area of the water into darkness. This makes nearby fish think, *Hey! There's a nice safe spot to hide out!* And as they swim closer to investigate, the herons use their stiletto-like beaks to summarily turn them into shish kebab.

That's a dirty trick to be sure, but that's no reason why you shouldn't head to the lake right now, umbrella and fire poker in hand, and bring home some goddamn dinner.

❯ "Herons and Egrets: Family Ardeidae," Naturia, naturia.per.sg

The world's largest mammal migration has nothing to do with those massive wildebeest stampedes you may have seen on some nature show. In fact, it doesn't even take place on the ground. It's bats—8 million of them to be precise. Every year in Zambia a veritable blizzard of 9-inch fruit bats called *Eidolon helvum* darkens the skies in leathery horror. And the flapping, squealing spectacle attracts predatory birds from far and wide to take part in the bat-eating murder bonanza.

All in all, it sounds like a good day to wear a hat.

> ❯"Fruit Bats: Africa's Greatest Mammal Migration," Discover Wildlife, discoverwildlife.com

The southern cassowary (*Casuarius casuarius*) of New Guinea and northeastern Australia is only the world's third largest bird (behind two species of ostrich), but comes in a landslide first place for murderous reputation. Thanks to a kick that's strong enough to shatter bone, along with dagger-like claws to serve as lacerating accompaniments to the kick, these blue-skinned, horny-headed, prehistoric proto-turkeys are perfectly capable of disemboweling any uppity human who encroaches on their territory.

But for those brave enough to tame this exceptionally violent bird, and who also have the foresight to bring along the proper ingredients, the rare but delicious dish of casso-turducken can be their hard-earned reward.

> ❯"Invasion of the Cassowaries," *Smithsonian*, smithsonianmag.com

A massive accumulation of bird poop was responsible for shutting down traffic in Nagano, Japan, a few years ago. According to the local power company, so many birds had been wantonly defecating on an insulator at one of their substations that the ensuing sludge caused a short circuit, resulting in an automatic shutdown that briefly brought the entire city to a halt.

It's unknown whether this was all an elaborate plan on the part of the birds, but nonetheless motorists were advised to remain in their vehicles and avoid looking up at all costs until further notice.

> ❯"Bird Poop Disables 25,000 Traffic Signals in Nagano," RocketNews24, via Yomiuri Online, rocketnews24.com

The sociable weaver (that's its actual name—its scientific one is *Philetairus socius*) is a bird that's known throughout Africa for building its nest not just during the breeding season but all year around. They are so dedicated to this endeavor that their creations can frequently get out of hand. By linking their contraptions together (and inviting other bird species to join their avian communes) their joint efforts sometimes result in structures so huge that they destroy trees and even send telephone poles crashing to the ground.

One can imagine the reaction of the first European colonists to visit Botswana and see a bird's nest the size of a Mack truck. And it must have been especially frustrating trying to get the thing to hold together after shooting it and nailing it to a mantel in the den.

❯ "11 Interesting Facts about Sociable Weavers," *Africa Geographic*, africageographic.com

❯ "House (Wrecking) Wrens," National Wildlife Federation, nwf.org

The house wren (*Troglodytes aedon*) is a drab-looking songbird that's abundant throughout the Western hemisphere. They're the most common type of wren, and are uncommonly cruel in their dealings with other birds. During breeding season, male house wrens will systematically destroy the nests belonging to any other bird species in the vicinity. And while they're at it, they're also sure to poke holes in the other birds' eggs, just to drive the message home.

Being that house wrens are small enough to fit in your hand, I wondered how they could possibly get away with being such vicious little jerks. But then I watched a retrospective on Joe Pesci's film career and everything cleared right up.

Most birds lay all their eggs at once so that the chicks grow up being the same size and leave the nest at the same time, thus improving their chances of survival. But a few birds, like some varieties of vultures and eagles, stagger it out and lay their eggs sporadically over the course of a few days. This often results in the oldest chick murdering the smaller, younger ones (80 percent of the time where golden eagles are concerned). And it's a handy system when food is scarce, since the older sibling can just make up for the lack of food by engaging in a little cannibalistic fratricide.

That's just a fancy way of saying, "They eat their baby brothers." Which just sounds cruel, horrible, and downright counterproductive to just about everyone, with the possible exception of Alec Baldwin.

❯*The Importance of Juvenile Cannibalism in the Breeding Biology of Certain Birds of Prey* by Collingwood Ingram

As many as 10 percent of all known birds have been able to mate successfully with species other than their own, producing chicks that are a hybrid combination of the two. Despite the moral implications inherent in such an activity, one can't help but wonder if they might be up to something. Like, maybe birds are sick and tired of being generally small and flimsy. Could they be trying to tinker with the evolutionary process, and perhaps be trying to screw their way into becoming dinosaurs again?

Whatever the case, if you've ever seen something that looks like a combination of an ostrich and a penguin, you'll probably be doing the world a service by shooting it immediately.

❯"The Amazing World of Hybrid Birds," Audubon, audubon.org

With their penchant for pounding away at trees,
you might suppose the way woodpeckers end the lives of the insects they're hunting for would be by way of their jack-hammering beaks. But it's actually their tongues that do all the dirty work. Woodpecker tongues are not just disturbingly long, but they are also shaped like spears (complete with barbs at the end), for use in skewering and retrieving even the most stubbornly entrenched prey.

> "*Melanerpes carolinus*: Red-Bellied Woodpecker," Animal Diversity Web, animaldiversity.org

Did I mention the screaming? Yeah, there's probably plenty of screaming going on as well.

Natterer's bat (*Myotis nattereri*), just like every single other member of their vile, flittering kind, has a very acute sense of hearing. This bat is pretty specific, though. Natterer's bat is able to hone in on the precise sound that flies make when they're having sex, which is its cue to immediately swoop in and ruin the flies' good time by gnashing them both to bits.

> "Caught in the Act: Bats Use the Sound of Copulating Flies As a Cue for Foraging," Phys.org, phys.org

I'm sure Mr. Natterer was a very fine fellow and all that, but I'm not sure that he'd be especially proud of having his name attached to such a murdering cockblocker.

Great Britain has been invaded by, of all things, parrots. Specifically, the very pretty rose-ringed parakeet (*Psittacula krameri*), which is rapidly spreading out of control and menacing crops with their pleasantly orange beaks. It's gotten to the point where the authorities are going onto private land without permission to wipe them out, and several instructional videos have been disseminated for the purposes of teaching people how to shoot them out of the sky.

> "Ring-Tailed Parakeets Are Flying Beyond Our Control," *Telegraph*, telegraph.co.uk

We can only hope that one of the videos is titled, "Polly Want Some Buck-shot?"

Bird strikes to aircraft cause over $600 million a year in damages, have caused 166 planes to make emergency landings since 2000 and are responsible for more than 200 human deaths since 1988. Aviation experts refer to the problem as Bird Aircraft Strike Hazard (BASH), probably because it just sounds cooler than "goose splats." The bloody collisions happen the most during takeoffs and landings but occasionally will occur when a plane is at peak altitude, with the highest recorded incident involving a Rüppell's griffon vulture (*Gyps rueppellii*) at an altitude of 37,000 feet in the air.

It can be difficult to trust a pilot who says the turbulence you just felt is nothing to worry about, especially when you look out the window and see vultures tracking your movements.

> "Birds Hit Planes Every Day, but Don't Usually Cause Crashes," ABC News, abcnews.go.com; "Roxie C. Laybourne, 92; Pioneer in Forensic Ornithology Aided Aviation," *Los Angeles Times*, latimes.com; "Bird Strike Hazards to Aircraft," AirSafe.com, airsafe.com

As anyone who's ever lived near the ocean knows, seagulls are jerks of the first order. But aside from the rampant theft and fecal carpet-bombing aimed at unwary humans, their unceasing torment can extend to innocent ocean creatures as well. Kelp gulls (*Larus dominicanus*) in Argentina have been annoying the local cetaceans for years, but they were just recently observed stepping over all lines of common decency by tearing the flesh out of the backs of baby southern right whales (*Eubalaena australis*) when they come up to breathe.

> "Horrible Gulls Are Eating Baby Whales Alive," *Discover*, discovermagazine.com

As reprehensible as the practice is of tossing antacids to seagulls to watch them explode (it doesn't work anyway), sometimes you have to think these seafaring shitheads are bringing it on themselves.

In 2002 the "Imagineers" at Disney World were forced to stop releasing pigeons at weddings and during the finales of some of their outdoor performances. It seems that a few opportunistic red-tailed hawks, knowing an easy meal when they saw one, were unnecessarily traumatizing children when the merciless raptors started swooping in and tearing the pigeons apart in full view of the audience. A spokesman explained, by way of a massive understatement, that "it wasn't fair to the pigeons to keep releasing them."

❯"Disney Ends Shows after Hawk Attacks," *Sun Sentinel*, articles.sunsentinel.com

After which an outraged Donald Duck presumably shook his fist at the podium while muttering a nearly unintelligible stream of profanities.

Rescuing an injured animal is certainly a noble thing to do, but you should always make sure beforehand that you're not dealing with a filthy ingrate. When a kind-hearted beachcomber in Wales noticed a Northern gannet (*Morus bassanus*) limping around in the surf in 2011, he quickly moved to assist the wounded bird, cradling it under his arm to protect it from the crashing waves. The gannet (*morus* is the Latin word for "stupid," by the way) repaid the man's kindness by pecking his eyeball right out of the socket.

❯"Man Blinded While Trying to Help Bird," *Independent*, independent.co.uk

The poor man now probably has to wear an eye patch. And even if he made the best out of the situation and became a swashbuckling pirate, he'd likely never be able to trust his parrot.

A highly accomplished paraglider was nearly killed in 2007 when two eagles attacked and almost sent her plummeting to the ground. Nicky Moss, described as Great Britain's top female paraglider was preparing for an event in Australia when she was set upon by two huge wedge-tailed eagles (*Aquila audax*). As Moss tells the story, the eagles attacked in tandem, tearing at the wings and her face, with one being especially determined: "It swooped in and hit me on the back of the head, then got tangled in the glider which collapsed it. So I had a very, very large bird wrapped up screeching beside me as I screamed back." By the narrowest of margins the eagle finally extricated itself and flew away, allowing Moss to breathlessly land the craft on terra firma.

What the story doesn't mention is whether or not Ms. Moss later celebrated her brush with death with a hearty meal of wedge-tailed eagle omelets made with the eggs she had previously stolen from the birds' nest.

> "Top Paraglider Attacked by Eagles," *The Sydney Morning Herald*, smh.com.au

In 2012 a swan attacked and killed a thirty-seven-year-old man in Chicago. He wasn't on a pleasure cruise but on the job as an employee of a company that actually used swans (and dogs) to keep bothersome geese off of homeowners' properties. The man was rowing out to check on the animals when one of the swans went ballistic for reasons unknown. The unreasonably angry bird first knocked him out of his kayak, and then continued to assault the poor man until he eventually drowned.

> "Killer Swan Blamed for Man's Drowning," ABC News, abcnews.go.com

Seeing as this incident took place in Chicago, we can't really blame the swan. Chances are it had already been robbed and shot by kayakers at least three times that year.

CHAPTER 3

Pernicious Parasites and Baleful Bacteria

At any moment of the day (and especially at night) you are practically guaranteed to have a multitude of unseen creatures crawling around, in, and on your person. The best you can do is to try not to think about it. But even when the unseen invaders aren't affecting you personally, they're tormenting some poor creature to distraction or, frequently, to death. But microscopic vermin and bacteria are one thing—sometimes the most baleful parasites are those that claim kinship with animals both large and small, from all across the creature spectrum. Stealing for a living is an activity that crosses all barriers, from the lowly mosquito to the mightiest tree. It's a proven route to success, as that mosquito would tell you if it could, "There's a bloodsucker born every minute." For example . . .

Hippopotamus rectums are a good source of blood, so maybe it makes sense that there's a parasite that's evolved to capitalize on that fact. *Placobdelloides jaegerskioeldi* is the scientific name of this South African leech, and it feeds on nothing else—just hippo butt. It begins the process by locating a leg, then slowly climbs its way up until it reaches its preferred target (which, to reiterate, is the hippo's butt). At this point there's nothing left to do except happily suck away for the rest of its days.

➤ "Um, This Leech Feeds on Hippo Rectums," *Wired*, wired.com

That scientific name isn't as descriptive as it could be. I'd have gone with "Tragicus stedmangrahamicus."

As far as we know, there aren't any leeches that specifically target humans, but it's not uncommon for waders to find one greedily slurping on an unprotected extremity after a dip in a river or lake. It can certainly be a harrowing, but not generally life-shattering, experience. Unless, of course, you're talking about a run-in with *Tyrannobdella rex*, the "tyrant leech king." They don't just latch on, but use their saw-like teeth to burrow into the orifices of mammals. It was only discovered recently, after one was removed from the nose of a little girl in Peru.

➤ "'Tyrant King' Leech Discovered, Attacks Orifices," *National Geographic*, nationalgeographic.com

We don't know much about this creature yet, but God willing we won't have to add the word "brain-devouring" somewhere in that name.

Amoebas in your swimming pool doesn't sound all that outlandish, at least until you find out there's one variety out there that can kill you by eating your brain. *Naegleria fowleri* is what they're called, and while they don't normally hang out in the local water park due to the chlorine, there's at least one case of someone accidentally snorting them after splashing around in a Florida apartment complex pool. He didn't make it.

Just one of a myriad of reasons why Florida is considered by many to be the nation's leading supplier of WTF.

❯ "Brain-Eating Amoeba Strikes in Summer," MedicineNet.com, medicinenet.com

The Congo floor maggot, apart from being a runner-up for having the least-flattering name in the universe, is the only known bloodsucking fly larva that feeds exclusively on mammals. Their mommy, a particularly vile species of blowfly (*Auchmeromyia senegalensis*), starts her children on the road to perdition by laying her eggs on the floor of inhabited huts. And once they become bouncing baby maggots, they'll spend the next ten weeks squirming along the floor, looking for bare feet.

I'll bet, right before this very moment, that you thought wearing fishermen's waders every day of your life sounded like a pretty stupid idea, huh?

❯ "The Congo Floor Maggot, *Auchmeromyia luteola* (F.) in a Laboratory Culture," by C. Garrett-Jones, *Bulletin of Entomological Research* (1951), journals.cambridge.org; *Physician's Guide to Arthropods of Medical Importance, Sixth Edition* by Jerome Goddard

The chronic disease known as bilharziasis sounds just as scary as the other name for the condition: schistosomiasis. But neither word is quite as terrifying as the common term for it, which is "snail fever." But it's not snails that invade your body; they're just another victim in this parasite's life cycle. It's worms. And once those worms get inside you (after you've carelessly gulped down some contaminated water), they'll hang out for as long as thirty years, having sex with one another and laying millions upon millions of eggs while they figuratively play kickball with your internal organs. What's not figurative, however, is how 200,000 people die from these wormy infestations each year.

❯ "Final Diagnosis—Schistosomiasis," University of Pittsburgh Medical Center, path. upmc.edu

Presumably some sufferers may choose not to seek treatment, as the worms seem to be having such a good time in there that removing them could be considered unconscionably rude.

Sea cucumbers (class Holothuroidea) seem to have an easy enough life, loafing around all day while also resembling a loaf of either some sort of moldy bread or rancid cheese. But their life of leisure is often thoroughly despoiled by a particularly rude type of fish. One that has no reservations about swimming straight up a sea cucumber's ass and devouring its gonads. Pearlfish (family Carapidae) are small (and mercifully narrow) nocturnal predators that have a hard time finding a place to hide during the day on the sandy open seabeds where they live. So they have learned to take advantage of neighboring sea cucumbers by treating them as impromptu shelter. Once inside, the unwanted houseguests live it up by having sex parties and sustain themselves by snacking on the cucumbers' genitalia. And in response, some cucumbers appear to be evolving a rather disturbing but useful defense mechanism: anal teeth.

❯ "This Fish Swims Up a Sea Cucumber's Butt and Eats Its Gonads," *Wired*, wired.com

What kind of sick joke was it to give these creatures a classy name like "pearlfish"? Unless the "pearls" they're talking about are those beads on a string that I . . . uh . . . heard about somewhere.

The human bellybutton, as fetching as some of them might look in a belly shirt, has been described by experts as "a rainforest of bacteria." Even if you routinely clean the thing, and no matter whether you're an "innie" or an "outie," it will still be a place where a wide assortment of filth will take up permanent residence. In 2012, a group of researchers published the results of an experiment in which they identified 2,368 species of both creepies and crawlies that were brand new to science.

However, in no way should this information encourage readers to approach strange women in bikinis and start talking about the filth in their holes.

> "1,458 Bacteria Species 'New to Science' Found in Our Belly Buttons," *The Atlantic*, theatlantic.com; "What Lives in Your Belly Button? Study Finds 'Rain Forest' of Species," *National Geographic*, nationalgeographic.com

Dracunculiasis (translated as "affliction with little dragons") is the appropriately horrifying Latin term that doctors use to describe a Guinea worm infection. It's a pretty accurate description too, considering it involves parasitic worms the width of "a cooked spaghetti noodle" wriggling around underneath your skin. You can get it by drinking dirty, water flea–infested water, and although you probably won't die, you might want to when you get to the part of the worm's life cycle when they poke their heads out of a blister they've created on your flesh.

> "Guinea Worm Disease Frequently Asked Questions (FAQs)," Centers for Disease Control and Prevention, cdc.gov; "Slaying 'Little Dragons': Guinea Worm Moves Toward Eradication," NPR, npr.org

Maybe you could make a game out of it to ease the tension. As you gently pull them out you can pretend you're a magician, pulling one of those endless ribbon tricks.

The "clean rooms" that NASA maintains to prepare equipment for space travel are probably the most sterile environments on Earth. These rooms are also the places where an extraordinarily hardy new species of bacteria, *Tersicoccus phoenicis*, was discovered a few years ago. What makes this even more startling is that the only other place these bacteria have ever been seen was in another clean room, 2,500 miles away. There's no explanation yet as to what exactly is going on, but that hasn't prevented NASA scientists from saying, "Screw it. We're sending this stuff into space."

❯ "New Bacterial Life-Form Discovered in NASA and ESA Spacecraft Clean Rooms," *Scientific American*, scientificamerican.com

And thus the first volley was fired in the centuries-spanning Intergalactic Germ Wars.

The sea lamprey is basically a leech that's 3–4 feet long. Unlike most leeches, which merely take a sampling of blood before dropping off back into the water, this fish latches on to a victim, mortally wounds it with circular rows of tiny, razor-sharp teeth, then pretty much drains it dry. It's been estimated that only about one in seven fish survives an encounter with them.

Which, admittedly, is better odds than most pet store guppies get after prolonged exposure to an eight-year-old.

❯ "Sea Lampreys, *Petromyzon marinus*," MarineBio, marinebio.org

The remora (Latin for "hindrance") has a "suction cup" on top of its head that it uses to attach itself to larger fish, whales, and occasionally boats. They're not parasites exactly—they're just so lazy and craven that they prefer hitchhiking to swimming around on their own. They're not complete cowards, however, as some have been shown to be bold enough to temporarily stick themselves right inside a shark's mouth. It's a reasonably fair trade, as the remora will clean off a few of the parasites from its host's skin, while the remora gets to feast on food scraps and then move back down to the other end to enjoy a steady stream of the larger organism's feces.

Leading to their other nickname, which I just made up: "the paparazzi fish."

> "Remora/Suckerfish," Project Noah, projectnoah.org

Toxoplasma gondii is a parasitic protozoan that resides in rats and cats. To get from the rat to the cat, the protozoan forms a cyst inside the rodent's brain that causes a very counterproductive (to the rat at least) change in its reaction to the smell of cat urine. Not only does the cyst remove its inherent fear of said rancid smell—the rat actually becomes sexually aroused by it. This leads to it becoming much less cautious in dangerous situations, thereby helping to accomplish *Toxoplasma gondii's* mission of getting inside a cat's stomach.

> "Cat-to-Rat-and-Back Parasite Directly Changes Human Brain Chemistry," The Wildlife News, thewildlifenews.com

Although even the hungriest cat might have some reservations about eating a rat that's furiously masturbating in its litter box.

Rats aren't the only ones getting their minds screwed with by *Toxoplasma* protozoa. They sometimes make their way into human brains as well, usually through contact with cat feces, and the condition it causes (toxoplasmosis) is the reason women should avoid litter box duty during pregnancy. Some early symptoms are flu-like in nature, and many may not even realize they're infected. Until the parasite starts eating away at their neurons, causing pesky little things like car crashes, suicidal tendencies, and schizophrenia.

Of course we can't rule out the possibility that this could all be a sinister plot by the psyops wing of Dog Fancy *magazine.*

❯ "How Your Cat Is Making You Crazy," *The Atlantic*, theatlantic.com

There are countless wasps that make life miserable for a number of other creatures. But there's one that stands head and thorax above the rest, at least in terms of brutally callous cruelty. The emerald cockroach wasp (*Ampulex compressa*) is a pretty, innocuous little thing, and one of the few wasps that don't automatically fill the average person with profound dread with their mere presence. But to cockroaches they are terror incarnate. Because when a female *Ampulex compressa* gets in a family way, the first thing she does is find a cockroach and insert her stinger directly into a very specific area of its brain. The wasp then injects a behavior-altering serum, leads her now-compliant victim to her lair, and lays a single egg on it. Soon, a larval wasp is born, which immediately burrows into the roach's flesh and begins feasting on its organs, one by one and in a way that prolongs its life as much as possible, until it eventually and mercifully expires.

How the heck am I supposed to make a joke about this without offending the long-suffering survivors of the Roach Holocaust?

❯ "The Wasp That Enslaves Cockroaches with a Sting to the Brain," *Wired*, wired.com

Wasps are generally such hideous parasites that it's nice to occasionally see them get some comeuppance. In this case, it's a fly providing the schadenfreude. Once a *Xenos vesparum* grub is able to get close enough to a paper wasp (*Polistes dominulus*) it will proceed to burrow underneath the wasp's carapace and do the normal routine of sucking out the innards. But that's just a warmup. The fly larvae will then alter the wasp's behavior, causing it to shun its nest mates and travel to another location where other infected wasps are compelled to congregate. If the grub is a male, the wasp will then simply be eaten and die while the grub transforms into an adult fly. But if it's a female grub, the wasp will be further manipulated into behaving like a queen, allowing it to infiltrate wasp colonies by impersonating royalty, whereupon the grub will then begin seeding the colonies with more parasites.

❯"Parasite Turns Wasps Into Outsider Zombie Queens," *Wired*, wired.com

It's definitely hard to know whom to root for in a situation like this. It's like going to a baseball game and being forced to choose between the Yankees and the Yankees.

The largest bacterium in the world was found in 1997, and it broke the former record for size by a factor of 100. *Thiomargarita namibiensis* is actually visible to the naked eye (you might mistake it for one of the periods on this page), and it's so big that other bacteria can live comfortably upon it.

❯"Thiomargarita namibiensis," Missouri University of Science and Technology, web.mst.edu

This can't be good news for the household disinfectant industry. Because who's going to want to clean their kitchen with a product that fills their house with tiny screams?

Slave-making ant is a catchall term that describes a wide variety of ant species that all do the very thing their name implies: make other ants their slaves. This sort of ant will invade the colonies of closely related species and literally force them to do their bidding (forage, tend to the usurper queen, and so on) upon threat of death. These oppressive insects have become so dependent on taking advantage of the hard work of others that they will actually starve to death without their slaves, even if surrounded by nearby food.

❯ "Slavemaking Ants: Taking Over the Colony," NC State University, ncsu.edu

Remember that story about the grasshopper and the ant, where the ant was portrayed as industrious while the grasshopper was painted as lazy? I think if the grasshoppers take this new evidence to court, they might finally win that libel lawsuit that's been dragging out for all these years.

And now let's have a little talk about the human botfly (*Dermatobia hominis*). You know, the filthy insect whose maggoty larvae burrow under your skin and grow fat on all the meaty goodness that lies beneath? Anyway, the way one contracts this loathsome condition isn't as simple as a botfly just laying a few eggs on your face—first it needs to torment a mosquito, a biting fly, or a tick, by seizing and laying its eggs on one of them first. The botfly then releases its minion to attack a human, and the hatching larvae then penetrate the skin via the tiny hole left by their servant's bite. And that's when the real party begins: having to carefully remove a stubborn maggot from your flesh, by whatever horrible means are at your disposal.

❯ "Couple Visiting Bolivia Became Infected with Flesh-Eating Botflies," ABC News, abcnews. go.com

Or maybe just leave it in there for a while as a conversation starter. Maybe even include it in a hilarious ventriloquist act at parties.

Coming down with a case of E. coli is not a pleasant experience in any way, but at least the condition can be treated with antibiotics. Well, at least it used to be. The summer of 2016 was when the first antibiotic-resistant strain of the bacteria became known to science, and hopefully the release of this book won't coincide with the impending E. coli apocalypse.

Not just because it would be bad for sales—thanks to the research I had to do for this, I already wound up spending a fortune on spider insurance.

❯ "The Superbug That Doctors Have Been Dreading Just Reached the U.S.," *Washington Post*, washingtonpost.com

The Western Australian Christmas tree (*Nuytsia floribunda*) is indeed a festive plant. But not really in a "peace on Earth, goodwill toward men" kind of way; it's more in the "off with their heads!" spirit of the French Revolution. In order to attack and parasitize surrounding trees, the roots of the Australian Christmas tree have evolved an appendage called a haustorium. This growth effectively works like a guillotine to slice a competitor's roots in two, after which the Christmas tree bonds its own roots to the open wound in order to steal the other plant's precious nutrients.

Let us all now bow our heads in silence, hold hands, and pray that Australia doesn't have a Halloween tree.

❯ "Western Australian Christmas Tree (*Nuytsia floribunda*)," Bioweb, bioweb.uwlax.edu

Carbapenem-resistant enterobacteriaceae

(which can mercifully be shortened to CRE) are also referred to as "nightmare bacteria." Not just because they kill 50 percent of those who get infected, but also due to their ability to shrug off just about every antibiotic known to man. CRE only recently appeared in the United States, in 2001, but their presence has reportedly been on the rise. And the "superbug" is now rearing its potentially cataclysmic head in 5 percent of U.S. hospitals, as well as 18 percent of long-term care facilities.

Worrying about global warming is all fine and dandy, but you just might be wishing for some warmer weather when the constant sweaty chills signal the coming of our new bacterial overlords.

> "'Nightmare Bacteria' Require Old and New Weapons," Live Science, livescience.com

The legend of the candiru, the Amazonian catfish

that anecdotal reports claim just loves to swim right up your urethra while you pee, doesn't really hold up to scrutiny. Or maybe it does, if you believe the guy who claimed one somehow traveled from the water, along the entire arc of his urine stream, and lodged itself in his peehole. At any rate, the fish we're talking about here (*Vandellia cirrhosa*) is actually plenty horrible on its own without all the penile invasion conspiracy theories. Scientists have confirmed that they will sneak into the gills of larger fish, sever an artery with their teeth, and then quickly engorge themselves on the gushing blood.

> "Would the Candiru Fish Really Eat Your Genitals?" BBC, bbc.com; "*Vandellia cirrhosa*: Candiru," Encyclopedia of Life, eol.org

But again, humans probably don't have much to fear from this fish. Unless you've had cosmetic surgery to have gills installed on your penis, which really only affects a very small percentage of the population to possibly include Nicolas Cage.

Kissing bugs aren't nearly as impishly whimsical as their name implies. They're actually a species of assassin bug. The reason they got that romantic name is because they like to suck the blood from your lips while you sleep. They're also transmitters of the parasitic protozoa *Trypanosoma cruzi*, which cause Chagas disease. In that scenario the pesky protozoa hide themselves away in your heart and digestive muscle—for years. And eventually, maybe once you've finally learned to live with chronic worminess, they'll cause you to die from a heart attack.

> ❯ "Chagas disease (American trypanosomiasis)," World Health Organization, who.int

Yeah, that was pretty bad. You might want to take a breather before we talk about the "heavy–petting cockroach."

Anelasma squalicola is a species of goose barnacle that attaches itself to various deep-sea sharks, and is the only barnacle in the world to be so bold. Once they're nice and snuggled in under a shark's skin, they send tendrils into the muscle tissue to suck out nutrients. And for no plausible reason other than to presumably shatter any self-confidence the shark may have left, the barnacles castrate it.

> ❯ "Caught in the Act: Phenotypic Consequences of a Recent Shift in Feeding Strategy of the Shark Barnacle *Anelasma squalicola*," by A. Ommundsen, C. Noever, and H. Glenner, *Zoomorphology* (2016), ncbi.nlm.nih.gov

Remember that old song about "Barnacle Bill the Sailor"? It was actually an allegory for the heartbreak of erectile dysfunction.

Another bastard of a barnacle goes by the name *Sacculina,* and its favorite devilish pastime is traumatizing crabs. Since they don't want the crabs to be wasting their harvestable energy on sexual pursuits, these barnacles also castrate their victims. But the humiliation doesn't end there. After removing its manhood, *Sacculina* will then change the crab's body so that it looks more feminine, and coerce him into performing sexy mating dances.

It wouldn't be so bad if it was something classy, but what if the poor crabs are being forced to even further debase themselves by undulating to the music of Michael Bublé?

❯"The Parasitic Barnacle *Sacculina*," Royal Society of Biology, blog.rsb.org.uk

---

Everyone knows that malaria is a horrible, mosquito-borne disease. And after the parasitic protozoa that cause it are finally done wreaking havoc inside your body (exploding blood cells and so on), they'll eventually need to move on to the next host before you become too sickly and withered to be of further use to them. But first they'll need to hitch a ride to get there. So, right before you die, the protozoa cause your body to emit a pleasant, lemony scent that smells simply delicious to . . . you guessed it: more mosquitos.

❯"Lemon-Scented Malaria," *National Geographic,* nationalgeographic.com

I suppose it's just like the gangsta rappers always say, "Don't hate the bloodsucking player, hate the multilayered parasitic game."

Should a snail have the bad luck to ingest the parasitic flatworm known as *Leucochloridium paradoxum*, the worm soon begins squirting out a succession of embryos into "fat, throbbing brood sacs," which are deposited in the snail's eyestalks. As the gestating worm babies pulsate and throb, the eyestalks turn bright green and start looking like something out of a sci-fi nightmare. Despite all that, this abominable sight looks irresistibly tasty to birds. So when one of them wolfs down the snail, the flatworms quickly take up residence and start laying eggs in their new host's rectum. This is so that future generations of parasites may be spread far and wide by traveling in the bird's poop.

That's a pretty awful process to go through just to get from one place to the next, but it's still probably not as bad as a Nashville-to–Las Vegas flight on JetBlue.

> ❯ "Infecting a Snail: Life Cycle of the Grossest Parasite," *Wired*, wired.com

When possible, a species of burying beetle (or "carrion" beetle) called *Nicrophorus pustulatus* will give birth to its loathsome larvae next to snake eggs. This is so that the grubs can burrow into the eggs, devour the unborn snakes, and then use the empty shells for protection. But sometimes there aren't enough snake eggs to go around, and so some grubs have to settle for growing up in a mouse corpse.

When the latter grubs were asked by the media about this outrageous example of housing inequality, the vast majority stubbornly refused to answer, while a few seemed to express their displeasure by vomiting mouse guts.

> ❯ "Host Shift by the Burying Beetle, *Nicrophorus pustulatus*, a Parasitoid of Snake Eggs," by G. Smith, S.T. Trumbo, D.S. Sikes, M.P. Scott, and R.L. Smith, *Journal of Evolutionary Biology* (2007), ncbi.nlm.nih.gov

There are some birds that make their living by robbing other birds, and the great skua (*Stercorarius skua*) may well be the reigning godfather of this dastardly ring of thieves. Like its cousins in the genus *Stercorarius* (Latin for "of dung"), the great skua is a "kleptoparasite" that thinks nothing of committing wanton acts of high-seas piracy. One of their favorite tactics (when they're not stealing chicks from nests) is to harass other seabirds in the air until the targets of their bullying are exhausted and forced to land. And then the skua harasses them further until they panic from the unrelenting abuse and vomit up their catch. Then, of course, the skua eats the vomit.

"Of dung"? Okay, granted, these aren't very nice animals. But you still have to think these birds might take some umbrage at the fact that science basically named them "shitbirds."

> "Sub Antarctic Skua, the Whale Bird," Ocean Blue Adventures, oceanadventures.co.za

---

If you've never had a bird defile your home, you may not realize just how revoltingly unclean they are. Most people have heard of the various forms of avian flu on the news. But in addition to that unpleasantness, birds (and especially what comes out of them) can carry more than sixty different types of infectious diseases. And that's on top of the fifty varieties of transmittable parasites that serve as a cherry on top of their fecal cake.

But I'm sure that those hot wings you're stuffing into your face are just fine. Go ahead, eat up, you disgusting reprobate.

> "Birds and Their Droppings Can Carry Over 60 Diseases," Medical News Today, medicalnewstoday.com

The roundworm called *Wuchereria bancrofti* is transported into the human body via mosquitos, which may not come as a huge shock. What's a little more alarming, at least if you're a guy, is what they can do to your balls. The worms can take up a year to fully develop into maximum horribleness, at which time they will take a journey throughout the various organs until they come to some lymph nodes. That's when your scrotum starts inflating like the world's most unpleasant and sporadically hairy party balloon, while your other extremities also swell to elephantine proportions. Which explains why the condition is called elephantiasis.

And which also explains why I'm never leaving the house again unless fully covered in Saran Wrap and a baseball cup.

❭ "Parasites—Lymphatic Filariasis," Centers for Disease Control and Prevention, cdc.gov

There is a strain of bacteria that is being kept in a lab at the University of Southern California that "eats" and "breathes" electricity. It's a little complicated to explain in the limited space we have available. But this particular bacteria, *Shewanella*, behaves so contrary to the rules of biology (and everything else that makes a lick of sense whatsoever) that scientists are seriously considering the possibility that it may be an alien life form.

Well, isn't that fabulous. We finally make contact with alien life and it's basically a case of athlete's foot that costs you money on your power bill.

❭ "Have We Found Alien Life?" *Popular Science*, popsci.com

The caterpillar of the Alcon blue butterfly (*Phengaris alcon*) is able to produce a smell that makes ants think it's one of their own grubs. This chicanery allows the caterpillars to enjoy a life of leisure as the ants neglect their own young in favor of wasting all their time feeding and tending to this fat, squirming imposter baby. It doesn't work every time, however. If the caterpillar doesn't get the chemical scent just right, the ants immediately tear it apart.

> "The Battle of the Butterflies and the Ants," *Nature*, nature.com

"It's absolutely worth the risk," Anna Nicole Smith was heard remarking from beyond the grave.

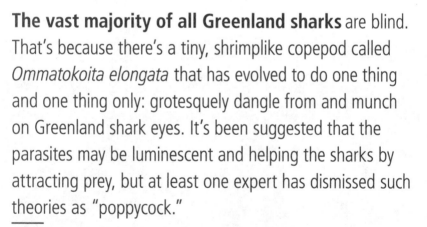

The vast majority of all Greenland sharks are blind.

That's because there's a tiny, shrimplike copepod called *Ommatokoita elongata* that has evolved to do one thing and one thing only: grotesquely dangle from and munch on Greenland shark eyes. It's been suggested that the parasites may be luminescent and helping the sharks by attracting prey, but at least one expert has dismissed such theories as "poppycock."

And in the stodgy world of zoology, when someone calls your idea poppycock, he's basically calling you a "stupid asshole."

> "Mysterious Giant Sharks May Be Everywhere," BBC, bbc.com

Even parasites aren't immune to parasites.

Creatures that survive by mooching off of other hitchhiking freeloaders are called "hyperparasites," and even they don't get the last laugh. It can get so ridiculous that there is such a thing as a "quinquenary hyperparasite," which would be a parasite of a parasite of a parasite of a parasite.

An example in human terms, I guess, would be something like Miley Cyrus's personal assistant's ne'er-do-well brother's drug dealer. Who, oddly enough, is rumored to be currently in talks with TLC about developing a new reality show.

❯*The Entomologist*, Volume 36, edited by Richard South, F.E.S.

The protozoan called *Leishmania* can be transmitted to humans by the lowly sandfly, and the infection it can cause (which would be leishmaniasis, naturally) will pretty much require that you take a sabbatical from your modeling career for a while. Because when these organisms (all twenty species of them) get into your face, they'll immediately cause the formation of an open sore that can last for years. There are plenty of other symptoms too, as well as different forms the disease may take. The most serious ones are called kala-azar ("black fever") and Dumdum fever, and the only parasitic condition that kills more people on a yearly basis is malaria.

Probably because when you have a scab for that long, it's next to impossible not to fiddle with it. Come to think of it, that's probably how that disease got named—doctors constantly having to remind their patients to "stop picking at it, dumdum." Actually, that name comes from a real town in India, in case you're looking for a fun addition to your passport stamp collection.

❯"Management of Trypanosomiasis and Leishmaniasis," by M.P. Barrett and S.L. Croft, *British Medical Bulletin* (2012), ncbi.nlm.nih.gov

A male twisted-winged parasite (a flying insect tormentor of bees) stabs his hooked penis into the female's neck to squirt his sperm directly into her body cavity. This makes a certain amount of sense, considering the heads of the females are the only parts that are visible. The rest of them is wedged inside the bodies of those aforementioned bees, which the parasites use as brood incubators.

❯ "Trauma in a Bee: Entomologists Shed Light on Bizarre Mating Mechanisms of Native Twisted-Winged Parasites," ScienceDaily, sciencedaily.com

So the next time you're stung by a bee, try to have a little sympathy. Because chances are you'd be pretty pissed off too if tiny hitchhikers were having prison sex on your back.

Deinococcus radiodurans **are the toughest bacteria on Earth,** and are able to survive a 15,000-gray dose of radiation. Just to give you a frame of reference, 10 grays would kill a grown man, and 1,000 would kill a cockroach. Extreme cold or dryness, acidity, and even the vacuum of space do little to deter this brute force of nature, and as a result scientists have nicknamed it "Conan the Bacterium."

Residents of California are even considering nominating the bacterium for governor on the platform, "Hey, it's not like it could make things any worse."

❯ "Extremophiles Act Like Alien Organisms," NBC News, nbcnews.com

The snuffbox mussel's (*Epioblasma triquetra*) method of reproduction is nastier than any tobacco habit, at least if you're one of the unfortunate creatures that happens to enter its domain. Because the method by which this mollusk has chosen to ensure the propagation of its species is to clamp onto the face of a passing fish, and then disgorge a copious amount of wriggling larvae down its throat.

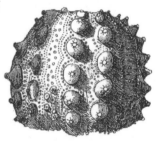

Imagine the nerve. All you want to do is go for a nice little swim and BAM! Suddenly you're an intern in the Clinton White House.

> "Snuffbox (*Epioblasma triquetra*)," Wildscreen Arkive, arkive.org

Trypanosoma brucei is the name of the protozoan that's spread by the bite of the dreaded tsetse fly, and is the parasite that causes the condition known as sleeping sickness. It certainly sounds like a relaxing way to meet your maker, and since it messes you up so badly that you might not have the wits to realize just what a dire situation you're in, maybe it is. But it's not so soothing for the people around you, who have to watch you develop nightmarish symptoms that essentially turn you into a zombie (sans the lust for brains) before you slip into a coma and die. You should be fine, just so long as you avoid places where tsetse flies live.

> "The Disease That Makes People Zombies," BBC News, bbc.co.uk

And avoid saying "tsetse" in general, unless you're absolutely sure how to pronounce it and can say the word without giggling.

When you hear that there's an actual, real-life, not-made-up-by-some-drunken-zoologist creature called a tongue-eating louse, you could be forgiven for assuming that a name like that couldn't possibly be an accurate description of said animal's behavior. Well, it's even worse than it sounds. *Cymothoa exigua*, a marine isopod and the rightful owner of the above moniker, is a fish parasite. And it does not eat fish tongues—it replaces them. After a louse enters a fish's oral cavity via the gills, it latches onto and cuts off the blood supply to the tongue, causing it to fall off. The louse then effectively becomes the fish's new tongue, getting first dibs on any food that its unwilling benefactor tries to eat. And to further show its disdain for its host's dignity, when a member of the opposite sex shows up the two parasites will engage in lousy coitus right there in the fish's mouth.

And you know they're probably all noisy about it too, giggling to themselves whenever the poor fish briefly interrupts their passionate lovemaking with its deep, heavy sobbing.

> ❯ "Tongue-Eating Fish Parasites Never Cease to Amaze," *National Geographic*, nationalgeographic.com

---

As if Siberia wasn't unpleasant enough, now they have to deal with parasitic, bloodsucking moths. Seriously. It seems that a former fruit-piercing moth of the *Calyptra* genus has discovered that its sharp proboscis is also great for penetrating human skin, and, as a bonus, its "bite" is reportedly much more aggravating than a mosquito's. It doesn't actually suck like a proper vampire, however. It prefers to slowly rock back and forth to drill its natural hypodermic needle deep into the flesh, and then just wait for its victim's blood pressure to do the rest.

Well, shucks. It looks like spending all my money on a Siberian timeshare condo wasn't such a good idea after all.

> ❯ "Skin-Piercing Blood-Sucking Moths I: Ecological and Ethological Studies on *Calpe eustrigata* (Lepid., noctuidae)," by H. Bänzinger, *Acta Tropica* (1975), ncbi.nlm.nih. gov; "Vampire Moth Discovered—Evolution at Work," *National Geographic*, national geographic.com

Most people know that cuckoos are jerks, laying their eggs in the nests of other birds so they don't have to deal with the hassle of chick rearing. But the various birds that wind up caring for cuckoo babies (which can quickly grow to be twice as large as they are) might not be doing it because they're just stupid and simply can't tell the difference. According to the "mafia hypothesis," taking care of a cuckoo chick may simply be part of a "protection racket," where the host birds are willing to deal with a little "brood parasitism," as this practice is called, to keep the cuckoos from barging in and wrecking their homes.

> "Fear of the Cuckoo Mafia: In Fear of Retaliation, Birds Accept and Raise Brood Parasites' Young," ScienceDaily, sciencedaily.com; "Thuggish Cuckoos Use Muscle to Run Egg Protection Racket," *New York Times*, nytimes.com

Well, I suppose the cold-case mystery of that sparrow I found with a tiny ice pick sticking out of its eye has finally been solved.

There's an insect called the cuckoo bee that engages in a particular brand of kleptoparasitism. The vestal cuckoo bee queen (*Bombus vestalis*) is especially notable for her violent audacity. This bee's standard modus operandi is to barge right into a hive of another species, head straight for her royal counterpart, and murder her right there in her chambers (along with any uppity worker bees who get in the way). After she so brazenly usurps the throne, the rest of the hive quickly fall in line and pledge their fealty. The remaining workers will then raise her children and remain loyal servants until such time as the new queen sees fit to release them from her service.

> "Vestal Cuckoo Bee (*Bombus vestalis*)," Wildscreen Arkive, arkive.com

In reality it's a little less Game of Thrones *than all that, but only because bees aren't very good at getting fire-breathing dragonflies to do their dirty work yet.*

Africa's Lake Tanganyika is home to a species of catfish named *Synodontis multipunctatus*. Also called the cuckoo catfish, cuckoo squeaker, or multipunk, it's a brood parasite. But the catfish has an approach that's a little more distressing than simply dropping off an egg in someone else's nest. The multipunk females lay their eggs inside another fish's mouth. It's not as crazy as it might sound, since the victims they choose (a type of cichlid) are "mouth brooders," meaning their mouths are where they raise their young. Anyway, as soon as the cuckoo catfish babies hatch, they introduce themselves by eating every one of the host's eggs, along with any non-cuckoo catfish babies that may have already hatched.

The real question here is, obviously, why in the world are they called "multi-punks"? Is it because they're awful on a variety of levels? The cichlids would probably agree with that.

> "A Brood Parasitic Catfish of Mouthbrooding Cichlid Fishes in Lake Tanganyika," by T. Sato, *Nature* (1986), ncbi.nlm.nih.gov.

The *Loa loa*, which causes the spectacularly unpleasant-sounding disease known as "African eye worm" is native to the rainforests of the Congo and Sudan. They use biting deer flies as their pathway to the inner squishiness of the human body, and once they gain entry, the worms nestle up in your fatty deposits and work their way up to your eyeballs. When they start forming cysts it can be painful, and when they die in there it can make for even worse news, but generally it's not catastrophic to either your eyesight or your life. The worst part about the *Loa loa* is you can actually see them, writhing around, every time you look in a mirror.

On the plus side, it'll be happy to ensure your victory in any staring contest.

> "Parasites—Loiasis," Centers for Disease Control and Prevention, cdc.gov

Don't think for a minute that putting in a pair of contact lenses will protect you from the threat of eyeball parasites. In fact, there's a type of amoeba called *Acanthamoeba* that will target you if you do. Once they get under your contact lenses, they'll eat away at your corneas, potentially causing permanent eye damage and even blindness. But don't worry; you can only contract them from bodies of water, soil, and the air. Um . . . okay, you can probably go ahead and worry.

Snorkeling masks should be fine, though. Go ahead and strap one on and head to the mall. If you don't get locked up for being a maniac, maybe you'll kick off a new hipster trend.

> "Acanthamoeba Keratitis FAQs," Centers for Disease Control and Prevention, cdc.gov

> "C Diff Smell—6 Key Facts for You," C Difficile, cdifficile.org

***Clostridium difficile* is a species of bacteria that causes severe diarrhea**, and is referred to as "*C. diff*" by hip medical workers in the know. But beyond that vexatiousness, the bacteria cause the stench of the discharge to become extraordinarily foul, to where it's comparable to baby poop, moldy bread, horse manure, and/or dead animals. It's a relatively common infection, and there's talk of training dogs to recognize the smell to assist in diagnosis.

If they knew that this is where they could end up should they flunk out, this information could do wonders for getting dogs to buckle down and do their homework in bomb-sniffing school.

Horsehair worms (*phylum Nematomorpha*) forcibly induce grasshoppers into becoming the first stop on their wretched, parasitic circle of life. Fish come next on the host list. So, to make sure the grasshopper that a horsehair worm is currently infesting gets gobbled up by a fish, the worm somehow takes control of the hoppity insect's brain and compels it to commit suicide. Which it accomplishes by jumping headlong into the nearest body of water. However, at this point an affected grasshopper is likely more than willing to embrace the sweet release of death, seeing as how at this stage in the process the wormy overlord inside its body has grown to several times as long as the grasshopper itself.

> ❯ "Parasitic Hairworm Charms Grasshopper into Taking It for a Swim," *New York Times*, nytimes.com

Now if these worms could just add an extra component and convince the fish to bite any fishing hook they see, weekends spent with Grandpa could become much less tedious.

Adactylidium, a tiny, parasitic mite, spends its life crawling on and eating insect eggs. Scientists were initially mystified when they discovered that the relatively few male mites they observed were dying almost immediately after being born, without even getting the chance to mate. What they discovered was that juvenile males have sex with their sisters inside the mother's body. So, once all the babies are ready to be born (by chewing their way through mom's corpse), the males have no reason to keep living.

> ❯ "Cicadas Aren't the Only Crazy Ones: Nature's Most Bizarre Life Cycles," *Wired*, wired.com

I guess nobody ever told them about the lucrative career they could have enjoyed in divorce law.

The poisonous Movile Cave in Romania contains life that has been completely isolated in total darkness for 5.5 million years. It was found in 1986, and in addition to the unique versions of blind spiders, leeches, centipedes, and scorpions that dwell within, the entire place is covered in a "floating mat of bacteria" that creates deadly levels of carbon dioxide.

The good news is that there's a nice, cushy surface in case you fall in a spelunking mishap. The bad news is you're dead and being nibbled apart by eyeless nightmares.

❯ "The Bizarre Beasts Living in Romania's Poison Cave," BBC, bbc.com

There's a fungus growing in the Brazilian rainforest that has the ability to bend ants to its will. *Ophiocordyceps camponoti-balzani* can somehow get inside and manipulate the brains of carpenter ants so that individual insects will wander off on their own, crawl to the underside of a leaf, and then bite down so that they're securely fastened. The ant then stays that way until it eventually dies. It is at this stage when the mushroom, having arranged for itself the perfect spot in which to grow, bursts right out of the dead ant's head.

❯ "'Zombie' Ants Found with New Mind-Control Fungi," *National Geographic,* nationalgeographic.com

We've been aware of the existence of this fungus for only a few years, but scientists already believe that they may have found a connection between it and the career of Shia LaBeouf.

***Onchocerca volvulus* is a filarial nematode, or roundworm,** that can get inside the human body after a bite from a black fly. Once they've made their arrival, they begin gradually spreading throughout the various organs, up to and including the eyes, in a hideous journey that takes as long as fifteen years. At some point the worms eventually do die, which is when the worst part happens. If any of the dead bodies start to decay in the vicinity of an infected person's eyeball, the result is blindness. And those worms that die elsewhere in the body can cause skin diseases with symptoms that have pleasant-sounding names, like "leopard skin" and "lizard skin."

Hopefully there will never be a superhero movie where the main character gets his powers from getting bitten by a radioactive nematode, because that might be the most disgusting thing to happen to the genre since Ben Affleck.

❭ "Onchocerciasis (River Blindness)—disease information," World Health Organization, who.int

***Pristionchus pacificus* is a nasty nematode,** and its host of choice is a certain type of scarab beetle. But it can be difficult for microscopic worms that live in the dirt to attach themselves to something as big as a fast-moving, armored insect. Luckily (for the worm, not the beetle), *Pristionchus pacificus* happens to be an extraordinarily crafty sort of parasite. In order to get high enough off the ground to be able to hitch a ride on a passing scarab beetle, the worms gather by the hundreds to form a writhing mass called a "worm tower," which snakes its way upward until at least one of them can grab hold of the beetle's belly.

❭ "A Thousand Worms Merge into a Living Tower," *National Geographic*, nationalgeographic.com

Which doesn't sound all that dissimilar to a method strippers might employ whenever a wealthy NBA player enters a gentlemen's club.

Ascaris lumbricoides is a roundworm that specializes in humans. You run the risk of getting them inside you whenever you make the bad decision to drink untreated water. Once one of their larvae squirrels its way into your bloodstream, it will move toward the liver and the heart, all the while growing until it reaches over a foot in length. Before that happens, though, the larva will enter the lungs and coerce you to hack it up and then swallow it again, in order to gain access to the small intestine, where it nestles in until it reaches maturity. And if you're thinking there's no way the existence of these things could ever affect you personally, you should probably know that 25 percent of the entire world's population has one inside them right now.

> ❯ "Parasites—Ascariasis," Centers for Disease Control and Prevention, cdc.gov

However, if you're looking for a low-maintenance pet and don't mind a little fecal-borne disease here and there, you could name one "Ropey" and plan a party for when it eventually emerges from your anus.

The oldest known cancer we're aware of is called Canine transmissible venereal tumor (CTVT).

It affects dogs, as you may have already guessed from the name, and it's only one of four known cancers that can be passed from one host to another like a parasite. It's pretty bizarre to think about a cancer that can hop from one creature to another, and it gets even weirder when you find out it can be transmitted not only like an STD but also when dogs merely sniff around each other's butts.

> ❯ "Canine Transmissible Venereal Tumour (CTVT)," Transmissible Cancer Group, tcg.vet.cam.ac.uk

Hopefully it never mutates to affect humans, because it's going to be hard for researchers to raise money for something called "doggy-style carcinoma."

The world's smallest fly, _Euryplatea nanaknihali_, makes up for its lack of stature with a flair for callous brutality. The way these tiny flies reproduce is by laying eggs in ants. And when the eggs hatch, the larvae immediately go to work chewing away at the ant's head, ultimately resulting in decapitation.

Thank goodness there's no comparable parasite for humans. Although as biological weapons go, I can't imagine getting much more psychological bang for your buck.

❭ "Do the World's Smallest Flies Decapitate Ants?" Entomological Society of America, entsoc.org

We recently discovered an entire genus of flies (_Dohrniphora_) that take a hands-on approach to ruthless decapitation. What happens is, one of these flies will land on an ant, use its bladed mouthparts to saw off the head, and then carry its prize back to the nest, where it will then lay eggs inside it.

❭ "Off with Their Heads: Flies Display a New Method of Decapitating Ants," _Entomology Today_, entomologytoday.org

"Hey! It's like they're making tiny Easter baskets!" is one way you might comfort a child after she returns from the garden, traumatized after using her new magnifying glass at the worst possible moment.

Just 50 grams of the bacteria known as *Clostridium botulinum* would be enough to kill every human being on the planet. It's also the same substance that people inject into their faces to remove wrinkles. But aside from how dubious a proposition "Botox" treatments are, and apart from the fact that it just might be the deadliest thing on the planet, let's talk about the new strain that was just discovered a few years ago that has no known antidote and requires just 13 billionths of a gram to eradicate you from existence.

❯ "New Botulinum Toxin Deemed Deadliest Substance Ever: Sniffing 13-Billionths of a Gram Can Kill," Medical Daily, medicaldaily.com

Actually, let's not. It would be much more fun to ask about whether or not there are any new awesome anthrax treatments to take care of all this fat in my ass.

There's an Asian species of mussel, *Anodonta woodiana*, that has made its way to Europe and is terrorizing the local fish population there with its parasitic larvae—particularly a local variety of bitterling fish named *Rhodeus amarus*. However, the fish have apparently become so fed up with their rude new neighbors that they decided to parasitize the mussels right the hell back. As a humiliating countermeasure, female bitterlings have learned to lay their eggs right in the mussels' mouths, with the male adding insult to injury by coming along later to squirt in a healthy batch of semen. The mussels, being mussels, can't do a damn thing about it and are forced to act as surrogate nannies for the next generation of bitterlings.

❯ "Bitterling Battle Between Parasite and Host," Earth Times, earthtimes.org

It's truly rare to hear about a nanny getting treated in such a manner outside of an Arnold Schwarzenegger divorce transcript.

Pubic lice (*Pthirus pubis*), or "crabs," can usually be found scurrying around the genitalia of the unclean and the uncouth. However, sometimes they can migrate outward from their unspeakable crevices, and might take up residence in one's armpits, eyebrows, mustache, and/or beard.

Therefore, the next time you consider getting romantic with a hipster, always be sure to check the iconic facial hair for unusual movement.

> "Parasites—Lice—Pubic 'Crab' Lice," Centers for Disease Control and Prevention, cdc.gov

No matter how clean you think you are, chances are that right now you have mites living on your face. They could be in your hair, your eyelashes, or buried in your skin. And they come out at night to crawl around and nibble on whatever detritus happens to be lying around.

A good strategy may be to eat a lot of Cheetos right before bed, just to make the greedy little bastards easier to spot and dig out in the morning.

> "You Almost Certainly Have Mites on Your Face," *National Geographic*, nationalgeographic.com

Remember that scene in *Stand by Me* where Wil Wheaton finds a leech on his "Lil Wesley"? Well, that unfortunate circumstance was apparently an occupational hazard for soldiers in Vietnam. Except merely finding one gorging on your testicle blood was probably preferable to how they would periodically slither right up some poor grunt's urethra.

If any conscientious objectors took the "self-inflicted penis leech injury" route to avoiding combat, I guess you'd have no choice but to admire their level of commitment.

❭*Stars and Stripes and Shadows: How I Remember Vietnam* by Tim Haslam

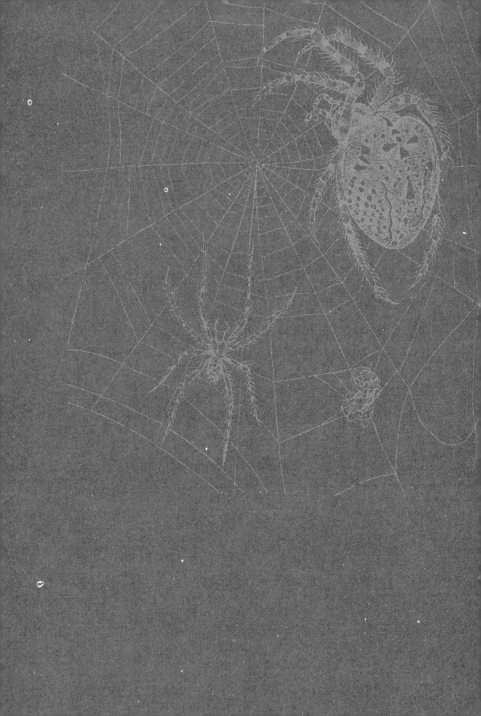

CHAPTER 4

Insidious Insects, Surreptitious Spiders, and Other Vindictive Vermin

If you think those with a spider- or insect-related phobia are making much ado about nothing, you are playing right into their hands. The insects and/ or the spiders, that is. Insects outnumber us 200 million to one, and if you were to weigh all the bugs in the Brazilian rainforest alone, the total mass would be greater than that of all the vertebrates on the planet. And if you feel emboldened by the fact that arachnids are much smaller than us, then you've never been trapped in a dank Laotian cave with a huntsman spider. "But we'd definitely be able to outwit them," you might mutter softly to yourself as you're rapidly surrounded by thousands of creatures able to attack and dismember on command in collective service to the hive mind. But after the countless tiny legs envelope you and the pain from the stings turns to numb acceptance, perhaps then you'll finally realize that the threat was always there, right in front of us. All we ever had to do was bend over, squint a little, and take a good hard look at . . .

Dracula ants (*Adetomyrma venatrix*) are even more horrible than Bela Lugosi in his heyday or even a shirtless pretty boy covered in sparkles. Sure, they suck the blood of the living and all that, but their victims of choice aren't supple yet pouty young virgins, but rather their own larvae. At least the little ant babies don't die, so that's . . . nice. We only recently discovered this species, and they're easily distinguishable due to their orange color and eerie resemblance to wasps. This aspect suggests to researchers that they may be a "missing link in ant evolution."

Yeah, either that or we finally found the guy who's been writing all those SyFy scripts.

❯"Dracula Ant (*Adetomyrma venatrix*)," Wildscreen Arkive, arkive.com

Some spiders mimic ants in order to eat them. It can be hard to get the disguise just right, however, since ants have three body segments while spiders only have two. One species of crab spider, *Aphanlochilus rogersi*, gets around this conundrum by first killing an ant that's wandered too far away from its friends. The spider then carries the corpse around and uses the dead ant's head to complete the disguise.

Coincidentally, that was one of the main "keys to success" in the unreleased book "Jeffrey Dahmer's Guide to Workplace Promotion."

❯"The Adaptive Bases of Ant-Mimicry in a Neotropical Aphantochilid Spider (Araneae: Aphantochilidae)," by P.S. Oliveira and I. Sazima, *Biological Journal of the Linnean Society* (1984), onlinelibrary.wiley.com; "If It Looks Like an Ant . . ." AntBlog, antweb.org

There's a species of assassin bug (*Acanthaspis petax*) that employs a camouflage strategy not only for infiltration but also perhaps to paralyze potential predators with horrified dread. This bug torments ants and sucks the life out of them, and then it gathers up to twenty of their corpses, binds them together with a sticky secretion, and wears the entire pile like a backpack.

> "This Insect Uses Its Victims' Carcasses as Camouflage," *Smithsonian*, smithsonianmag.com

It's theoretically possible that the bugs may be engaging in this behavior out of some twisted sense of fashion, in which case PETA should consider staging a few of their outraged protests over in the Malaysian jungle.

Like it or not, just about everything you eat includes a certain amount of bugs (or at least parts of them) that aren't mentioned in the list of ingredients. In fact, the FDA has decided on an "acceptable" amount of insect fragments that can be found in almost every food product you buy. For example, fruit juices are practically guaranteed one maggot per every 250 milliliters, and cornmeal comes complete with at least one whole bug per 50 grams. Also, should you be one of the people I've never met who buys "fig paste" on a regular basis, you're gobbling down thirteen insect heads for every 100 grams.

> "The Food Defect Action Levels," U.S. Food and Drug Administration, fda.gov

On the bright side, you can make your coworkers think you're a total party animal because you "ate the worm" last weekend, when all you actually did was sit around the house, alone in a robe, drinking glass after of glass of sad, lukewarm homemade mimosas.

There are a few spiders that curl up in a ball and flop down a hill to avoid predators, but the Moroccan "flic-flac" spider (*Cebrennus rechenbergi)* is the only arachnid that can tumble down and even up sand dunes, completely under its own power. Its unique method of locomotion impressed scientists enough that they're now building space robots based on the flic-flac's design. Flipping end-over-end all day can take a toll, however, and if they cartwheel around for too long they can actually die from overexertion.

❯"A Desert Spider with Astonishing Moves," *New York Times*, nytimes. com; "Cartwheeling Spider Found, Inspires New Robot," *National Geographic*, nationalgeographic.com

Great. Leave it to spiders to take all the sexiness out of gymnast–related exhaustion.

The Amazonian giant centipede (*Scolopendra gigantea*) is so big it can eat bats. And instead of taking the easy way out by simply creeping up on the bats while they sleep, the multi-legged, 12-inch goliaths employ a much more devious method. After securing themselves onto a cave roof with their rear legs, they proceed to dangle directly in the middle of the bats' flight path, and snatch them from the air as they pass.

And that's why rule two of spelunking is "don't look up." I think rule one has something to do with how you shouldn't lick the walls.

❯"Amazonian Giant Centipede (*Scolopendra gigantea*)," Wildscreen Arkive, arkive.com

Camel spiders (order Solifugae) aren't spiders at all, but somehow they manage to be twice as terrible. Their monstrous jaws can be up to one-third of the entire length of their already impressively ghastly bodies, and that's just for starters. In addition, since they're not venomous, their jaws operate in a unique way. Once they get ahold of prey (which can include plaintively squeaking rodents) they use their jaws to grind their victims into pulp while their digestive juices do their part to liquefy the flesh.

❯ "Camel Spiders: Facts & Myths," Live Science, livescience.com

Which might explain why so many of the Iraq War veterans return home and speak in hushed whispers about "The Valley of Lost Toes."

The "Komodo dragon" of wasps was discovered just a few years ago on the remote island of Sulawesi, and was quickly given the Godzilla-nemesis-sounding title of *Megalara garuda*. The fact that they're as large as a mouse is pretty disconcerting, but that happens to be only the second most horrific thing about them. Number one with a bullet would be the fact that the jaws on the males of this species are longer than their limbs, and are so impossibly gigantic that they wrap around the wasps' heads. On a positive note, the only specimens found thus far have all been dead.

❯ "Bizarre 'King of Wasps' Found in Indonesia," *National Geographic*, nationalgeographic.com; "Meet the Just Discovered 'Komodo Dragon' of Wasps," Mongabay, news.mongabay.com

At least if these guys show up at your picnic, you could try and convince one to help pop open a few bottles of beer.

We think of spiders as solitary hunters, but a recently discovered species of long-jawed orb weaver (family Tetragnathidae) was observed living together in cooperative communities like dirty hippies. Unlike hippies (well, except for those famous ones who did some stuff in Los Angeles back in the 1960s), they seem to be hunting in packs. This unsettling news was stumbled upon when some poor sap wandered into a web the size of a football field in North Texas.

So far researchers claim these spiders are completely harmless. Yet somehow I doubt those "long jaws" are used for playing bongos at Grateful Dead concerts.

❯"Massive Communal Spider Webs Cover Trees in Dallas Suburb," UPI, upi.com

You don't necessarily need a shiver-inducing conglomeration of spiders to get a gargantuan web. There's one species that can build a silky contraption that's 82 feet across, all by its lonesome. The web of the Darwin's bark spider (*Caerostris darwini*) is just one of many reasons why a trip to Madagascar is best spent entirely in a hotel room, and aside from just being big, the web's individual strands are reportedly stronger than a Kevlar bulletproof vest.

❯"World's Biggest, Strongest Spider Webs Found," *National Geographic*, nationalgeographic.com

Not to suggest that wildly firing a machine gun at anything that moves isn't a perfectly appropriate response when encountering a spider web that's the size of a regulation basketball court.

Reportedly, H.R. Giger (the maniac responsible for creature design in the original *Alien* movie) got the idea for the monsters from an unlikely source: dragonfly nymphs. Because, holy crap, they have the look going on. But at least Giger was considerate enough to not incorporate other unusual features that dragonfly larvae have. Chief among them being the ability to breathe from their anuses and zip around via squirty, butt-powered propulsion.

Yeah, I'm not sure that many sequels would have been in store if the film's antagonist kept announcing its presence with a sudden "BLAPBLAPBLAP-pfffffftsqueak!"

❯ "There are aliens among us," *Guardian*, theguardian.com

New Zealand's Wetapunga (*Deinacrida heteracantha*) looks like a cricket with a glandular disorder

(*Deinacrida* is Greek for "terrible grasshopper"). They can grow as large as a gerbil, with the females being much bigger than the males. They don't have wings (proving that nature can occasionally be capable of granting small mercies), but they do have powerful mandibles and holy hell yes they can bite. Moreover, they can kick like a bastard and inflict grievous wounds with their spiny legs. It's definitely the largest, but it's only one of the seventy different species of weta that are currently scuttling about New Zealand. You can find them in caves, trees, and home gardens, and generally crawling around on the ground almost anywhere you go.

Wait, weren't The Lord of the Rings *movies filmed in New Zealand? And did the weta population rise up in protest when they found out Shelob wasn't actually the star of the movie?*

❯ "This Bug Is Big as a Gerbil. Fortunately It Loves Carrots," *Wired*, wired.com

The award for the insect with the most toxic venom doesn't go to a spider or scorpion (partially because neither is an insect), but an ant. Maricopa harvester ants to be precise. Not only can just one of these tiny, bad-tempered bugs inject you with a cocktail of potentially deadly poisons, but they also emit pheromones to alert every other harvester ant in the vicinity to join in on the fun, and to provide a signal when they should all bite in unison.

It's like a fun game of Simon Says, only with more death by ant poison.

❯"Chapter 23: Most Toxic Insect Venom," *Book of Insect Records*, University of Florida, entomology.ifas.ufl.edu; "Recruitment pheromone in the harvester ant genus *Pogonomyrmex*," by B. Hölldobler, M. Inwood, N.J. Oldham, and J. Liebig, *Journal of Insect Physiology* (2001), researchgate.net

Assassin spiders have long necks, which is a bodily feature one normally wouldn't associate with arachnids. That unsettling detail, along with their absurdly outsized jaws, gives them such an outlandish appearance that some people refer to them as "pelican spiders." And that's an even more appropriate comparison when you consider how brutal pelicans can be, as discussed in Chapter 2. Anyway, as goofy as assassin spiders may look, both of those aforementioned anatomical aspects are essential in helping them keep their distance from their favorite prey: other spiders.

Just another thing you might want to keep in mind before you start making fun of that awkward kid on the playground whom everyone refers to as "Timmy the Pelican."

❯"Spider-Killing Assassin Spiders," Earth Archives, eartharchives.org

Caterpillars have it rough, especially if they don't have great camouflage or at least a poison filling to ward away hungry birds. Another threat they face is the scourge of parasitic wasps, a predator that often tracks caterpillars by following their trails . . . of poop. In response, skipper butterfly caterpillars (family Hesperiidae) have learned to cover their trails (or do away with them altogether) by launching their turds with specialized butt catapults. Indeed, evolution was actually kind enough to provide these caterpillars with anal "launch pads," capable of firing their frass (that's tech-speak for "bug crap") a distance of up to 40 times their body length up, up and away.

For reference, that's like if you or I had a bowel movement that flew well over half the entire length of a football field. Which would come in pretty handy for a very unorthodox but satisfying crime-fighting career.

> ❯ "Scat-Firing Caterpillars Elude Predators," *National Geographic*, nationalgeographic.com

An insect that's become adept at weaponizing its own dookie is the tortoise beetle.

Some, like *Cassida viridis*, make good use of their "highly elongated and mobile anus" to fashion "fecal shields," which can be wielded in defense or as the bug equivalent of a mighty battle-axe. And then there are the larvae of the sumac flea beetle (*Blepharida rhois*), which simply keep shitting all over themselves until they're fully ensconced within a feculent force field that's vile enough to make most predators think twice before making a snack out of them.

> ❯ "This Beetle Uses Its Poop as a Shield or Sword," *Wired*, wired.com; "By the Power of the Poop-Shield: Beetle Defences of the Faecal Kind," Earth Touch News Network, earthtouchnews.com

---

Actually, most predators probably only think once. And that thought would be "nope."

It may sound like something out of a dystopian sci-fi movie about the Robot Apocalypse, but in 2013 we discovered the only known insect to have working "gears." *Issus coleoptratus*, a species of planthopper native to Europe, Asia, and northern Africa, has structures on its hind legs that look like they were ripped off a very, very tiny bicycle. They're part of a system that allows the bug to leap great distances, and the teeth on the "gears" line up to ensure that the legs fire off in unison, thus preventing the planthopper from spiraling out of control after launch.

I, for one, welcome our new cybernetic insect overlords. Plus, when you smack them with a rolled-up newspaper, you can gather up all the parts and make a tidy profit by selling them to unscrupulous watch repairmen.

❯"This Insect Has the Only Mechanical Gears Ever Found in Nature," *Smithsonian*, smithsonianmag.com

Further evidence of an impending insecto-cyborg uprising can be found in the fig wasp *Apocrypta westwoodi*, which essentially has a metallic "drill bit" on its ass. These fruit-sucking wasps are rather tiny, and it can be hard for them to pierce through the tough skin surrounding the average fig (which they need to do in order to eat and lay their eggs). So Mother Nature decided to bestow upon them a stabbing implement called an ovipositor, which is thinner than a single strand of human hair but harder and sharper than the ghastliest of dental equipment. All thanks to a generous coating of zinc on the tip.

❯"Wasp Bores into Fruit with Metallic 'Drill Bit,'" *National Geographic*, nationalgeographic.com

Surely it's only a matter of time before these insects realize that the hypodermic needle they have at their disposal can do a lot more than just puncture fruit. At which time the name "fig wasp" will probably need to be replaced with something like "the toddler-impaling mecha hornet."

You know how awful it is when you walk into the kitchen in the middle of the night, flip on the light switch, and see cockroaches skittering back to their hidden lairs? Well, imagine a scenario in which you surprised them like that, and they had the ability to jump. In 2006 we discovered that there is indeed a roach that can leap like a grasshopper, and they might even be able to do it better. *Saltoblattella montistabularis* can only be found in South Africa right now, so perhaps you needn't be concerned about how they can hop nearly fifty times their own length with spring-loaded legs.

❯ "Leaping Cockroach Gets Around on Spring-Loaded Knees," *Wired*, wired.com

But you might want to consider dumping all of your money into roach motel stock in preparation for the coming invasion, just in case.

Did somebody say "bizarre cockroach variants"? Well, how does one that lives in volcanoes and glows in the dark grab you? The enigmatic vermin in question is called *Lucihormetica luckae*, and looking at one from above is uncannily reminiscent of the Jawas from *Star Wars*, complete with the luminescent eye-thingies. They indeed make their home in active volcanoes, which may have been a poor evolutionary strategy, in retrospect. Because researchers believe they may have been wiped out immediately after they were first discovered, within the bowels of Ecuador's Tungurahua volcano in 2012, when an eruption turned them all into ash.

❯ "Volcano Vaporizes Cool Glowing Roach," Seeker, seeker.com

On the next episode of "Intelligent Design Bloopers," we'll show you a frog whose mating call sounds exactly like a "yo mama is so fat" joke, spoken in the language of snakes.

Over the past few years we've been discovering a large amount of new tarantula species in South America. And worse, from the looks of them, they may be evolving specifically to lure children. From pink to purple to blue, along with stripey combinations in between, many of the new species discovered have been inexplicably colorful. And with their inherent furriness, it's easy to see how a child might mistake one for a plush toy and end up with a pair of fangs violently entering his face. It's obviously not camouflage—and "taffy-colored" doesn't exactly shout, "Warning! Do not touch!"—so what the heck are these arachnids up to?

❯"Nine Colorful Species of Tarantulas Found in Brazil," Sci-News.com, sci-news.com

Seriously, it's like they consulted with clowns to come up with the mother of all phobias.

There are plenty of tarantulas in the United States too, and every year during mating season they migrate in unison with a singular purpose over the western desert, crossing highways and sometimes through people's homes. Apparently the safest place to be is in an eighteen-wheeler, because some of the lonely stretches of road that truckers frequent will become scenes of mass, spidery carnage, as the tarantulas carpet the asphalt and end up the victims of vehicular genocide.

❯"Tarantulas on the March," DesertUSA, desertusa.com; "March of the Tarantulas," SoCal Wild, socalwild.com

You know what's another safe place to be? Anywhere that tarantulas aren't.

Since neither ants nor wasps are native to the islands of Hawaii, another mighty and fearsome creature has emerged to fill the niche of über–insect predator: caterpillars. In fact, the Aloha State is the only place in the world you'll find caterpillars that behave more like Bengal tigers than their fat, squirmy cousins. With front legs that have evolved into grasping claws and mouthparts that can chew on a whole lot more than just leaves, the larvae of the *Eupithecia* genus do a good job of reminding us (or at least flies) that even paradise can be a place of unremitting brutality.

You should see the moths they turn into. I'm pretty sure they look like giant bats and attack tourists by the hundreds every year with bloodthirsty impunity and then turn them into werewolves or something. But I could be very, very wrong.

> "Hawaiian Carnivorous Caterpillar—*Eupithecia*," Hawaiianforest, hawaiianforest.com

There are bigger and more venomous ants that live in the jungles of the Amazon. However, no other ant displays behavior that bears a greater similarity to the tyrannical despots of old than the scrawny, yellowish-orange species called *Allomerus decemarticulatus*. Because none of them builds elaborate torture chambers to torment its enemies. These ants are able to capture prey much larger than themselves by manipulating the fungus on trees, creating tiny holes for other insects to step into. Once they're caught, the ants will grab hold, sight unseen, and stretch them out while their cohorts sting the immobilized victim repeatedly until it dies.

> "'Torture Racks' Are First Known Traps Made by Ants," *National Geographic*, nationalgeographic.com

Presumably while an evil ant queen watches from a distance, rubs her front legs together, and whispers, "Yessss. Yessss."

A brand new species of the abomination that is the forcepfly (family Meropeidae) was just recently discovered in 2013, and that now makes three thrilling species named after invasive surgical equipment to choose from. Science doesn't know much about them yet, but judging by their appearance, the prospects don't look very good. About all researchers do know at this point is that they, like all male forcepflies, have a mammoth set of intimidating genitals, and they're shaped like pincers.

But maybe I'm being unfair here, and those "pincers" are actually for giving each other long, romantic hugs. Sure, why not? Also, I would very much like a drink.

❯"New Insect Discoveries: Forcepfly with Terrifying Genital Pincers and Tinkerbella, the Minute Fairyfly," *Scientific American*, scientificamerican.com

For many male spiders, sex is a delicate dance with death. Since romantic encounters often end with the females chewing their heads off, it's not really in a male's best interest to stick around for snuggling. So, to hurry the process along and hopefully avoid falling victim to post-coital cannibalism, the orb-web spider *Nephilengys malabarensis* has developed a tactic that is drastic yet prudent. It detaches its penis right in the middle of the act, and then it runs like hell.

While making a resolution to never look for a date on Spider Craigslist ever again.

❯"Spider's Detachable Penis Finishes Without Him," Live Science, livescience.com

In 2015 explorers in the Peruvian Amazon happened across a caterpillar belonging to an as yet unknown species of moth. When circumstances arose that caused one of the researchers to yell (such circumstances being abundant in the Amazon), the mysterious caterpillar responded to the loud noise by unfurling four long tentacles. The purpose of having spring-loaded tentacles that respond to human screams, much like the identity of the caterpillar itself, remains an ominous conundrum.

As of now scientists are referring to the creature as the "tentacle caterpillar," and thereby missing a great opportunity to give it a much more descriptive and foreboding moniker: "Face Hugging Cthulhu Spawn."

❯ "Bizarre Caterpillar with Erupting Tentacles Filmed," *National Geographic*, nationalgeographic.com

---

Even if you're so committed to avoiding ants that you insist on traveling all the way to the Sahara Desert for picnics, there's a good possibility they'll still come after your sandwiches. And chances are it will be the Saharan silver ant (*Cataglyphis bombycina*), a species that earned that name because they really do look like they're made out of silver. You can't actually melt them down for jewelry, however (sorry to ruin your anniversary plans). The reason silver ants developed their metallic sheen is because it helps to protect them from sunlight. And combined with their extra-long, spidery legs to keep them off the hot ground, this makes them perfectly capable of foraging for your macaroni salad even in extreme heat.

❯ "Silver Ant Hairs Reflect Sunlight, Keeping Sahara Dweller Cool," *Science News*, sciencenews.org

---

If you think this adaptation sounds pretty neat, just think of the sadness of the poor children who mistakenly try to torment these ants with a magnifying glass, and then have their corneas fried out by the reflection.

You decide the best way to have a bug-free picnic is to head to New York and set out a blanket right in the middle of a snowstorm. But you're screwed there too. Not because of something crazy like snow ants, but because of something even crazier: flies with "antifreeze" in their blood. There are a few insect species, like the winter stonefly (family Capniidae), that can tolerate the kind of extreme cold that would give a polar bear shrinkage. They've evolved a way to prevent ice crystals from forming inside them when the temperature drops, allowing them to be annoying the whole year round.

❯ "Winter Stoneflies Sure Are Supercool," *Scientific American*, scientificamerican.com

Great. Winter used to be the one time of year I could skip my monthly shower/underwear swaps. Thanks for breaking my cover, flies.

Australia's a pretty scary place where the local fauna is concerned. From the deadly snakes and dog-sized spiders to the man-eating sharks and knife-wielding koalas, simply making it home in one piece must be a relief for the average Aussie. And that's when they find out just how much nature hates them—when they sit down to relax with a cold one but can't, because there's a beetle having sex with the bottle. The Australian jewel beetle (*Julodimorpha bakewelli*) to be precise. Because a local distillery was distributing bottles (called "stubbies") that were the exact color of a female jewel beetle in heat, the males couldn't restrain themselves from dry humping their product to completion.

❯ "Nature Mimics: Why Bugs Mate with Beer Bottles," *Australian Geographic*, australiangeographic. com.au

"Oy, mate. This beer you just gave me seems a mite frothier than usu . . . Oh crikey."

Everybody knows that fiddling around with a scorpion is a colossally bad idea, but one in particular can ruin your day in a uniquely terrifying manner. The South African spitting scorpion has a stinger that contains a cocktail of three different poisons that it can deploy for different purposes. After first spitting (yes, spitting) a sample load in the general direction of its chosen victim, it releases follow-up poisons that can cause symptoms such as "tremors, convulsions, profuse salivation, lacrymation, continuous urination and vocalization."

❯ "Three Structurally Related, Highly Potent, Peptides from the Venom of *Parabuthus transvaalicus* Possess Divergent Biological Activity," by B. Inceoglu, J. Lango, I. Pessah, and B.D. Hammock, *Toxicon* (2005), researchgate.net

"Lacrymation" is just how serious people in lab coats say, "crying," in case you were wondering. But I guess "pissing yourself, drooling, and shrieking in a fit of spastic tears" doesn't go over very well in scientific journals.

An even worse idea would be getting up close and personal with a deathstalker scorpion (*Leiurus quinquestriatus*). Their name pretty much says it all. But even with a totally metal name like that, they're still not the world's deadliest of their pinchstabby kind. The Indian red scorpion (*Hottentotta tamulus*) gets the gold medal for that. Their poison causes an array of symptoms that read like a to-do list for torture demons in the seventh circle of hell, and the fatalities they cause mostly involve women and children.

❯ "Deathstalker Scorpion—*Leiurus quinquestriatus*," ScorpionWorlds, scorpionworlds.com; "Utility of Scorpion Antivenin vs Prazosin in the Management of Severe *Mesobuthus tamulus* (Indian Red Scorpion) Envenoming at Rural Setting," by H.S. Bawaskar and P.H. Bawaskar, *Journal of the Association of Physicians of India* (2007), japi.org

The "Indian" in the name refers to the country, not Native Americans. Which is good because that sounded a little racist. Which means it would be a great choice for the name of the next NFL expansion team.

The bite of the Australian funnel web spider is widely considered to be one of the worst things that can happen to a person. Oddly enough, the neurotoxin in their fangs is completely harmless to just about every type of mammal except primates. When a human gets a dose of what the funnel web spider is packing, death can occur in as little as fifteen minutes from cardiac arrest or pulmonary edema. That last one is when the capillaries in the lungs start to explode, causing said lungs to fill up with fluid, followed by victims eventually dying by drowning in their own juices.

———

Considering the fact that there are no primates in Australia except for humans, one might begin to believe in the possibility that entire continents can sometimes just be assholes.

❯*Funnel-Web Spiders* by Jill C. Wheeler

The Amazon has a competitor in the race for most horrible death by spider. Several, in fact. When a member species of the genus *Phoneutria* (of which there are six), also known as Brazilian wandering spiders, sinks its fangs into a man's flesh, one of the first things he can expect is to immediately get a massive erection. This is not as much of a pleasant surprise as it may sound. Because the poison can cause the poor guy to lose muscle control in his respiratory system, resulting in a rapid death by suffocation.

Which is just one of a myriad of reasons why you should never buy boner pills off the Internet that have tarantulas on the package.

❯"Natural Viagra: Spider Bite Causes Erection," Live Science, livescience.com; "Brazilian Wandering Spider," Bioweb, bioweb.uwlax.edu

The larvae of *Brachyspectra fulva*, or "Texas beetles," lie flat like a rug and secrete a scent that's quite enticing to spiders. It sounds like a death wish on the part of the grubs, to be sure. But once a spider is lured into range, they pierce the hapless arachnid with a nail-like tail, pinning them to their backs. And then, you know, the regular stuff happens. Brutal evisceration and all that jazz.

A grub that kills and eats spiders doesn't make a lot of sense, but then again it is from Texas. Heck, they might even do it while wearing a silly hat.

❯ "Review of the Family Brachypsectridae (Coleoptera: Elateroidea)," by C. Costa, S.A. Vanin, J.F. Lawrence, S. Ide, and M.A. Branham, *Annals of the Entomological Society of America* (2006), branhamlab.com

You know those cute little water bugs you see skittering in ponds? Well, the biggest version of them can grow to over 4 inches long, are able to fly, and can also inject you with a digestive enzyme that can leave you with permanent muscle damage. The family of insects they belong to is called Belostomatidae (also "toe biters," because of their agony-inflicting beaks), and the giant ones are considered the planet's largest true bugs.

❯ "The Attack of the Giant Water Bug," *Scientific American*, scientificamerican.com

They're probably very smug about it too. But let's just let them have this one. It's not like bugs get a ton of reasons to feel good about themselves anyway, and it might do wonders for their overall self-esteem.

***Camponotus cylindricus* ants hail from Borneo,**
and have a defensive strategy that puts the most hardened
terrorist to shame. When under threat, they'll grab on to
an attacker with their jaws, and then constrict their abdominal muscles so hard they literally explode. Which
causes the noxious "yellow goo" that was formerly contained in their abdomens to spray in all directions.

*So if this ant shows up at your picnic, at least you can poke it with your sand-
wich to add a little zesty sauce.*

❯ "The Original Suicide Bombers? Borneo's Exploding Ants Commit Suicide to Protect Colony," *Discover*,
discovermagazine.com

Leopard slug sex is a highly complicated affair,
mainly due to the fact that both parties must carefully maneuver their gigantic blue penises. Said penises are nearly
as long as the slugs themselves, and the fact that leopard
slugs are hermaphrodites means everyone at the party has
them. In order to facilitate their delicately majestic phallic
dance, two slugs will begin the process by exuding a large
amount of goo, after which they "descend on a slimy rope"
so that they're both hanging upside down. It is at this point
that the blue penises emerge from the right side of their
heads. The slugs will now intertwine their penises into a
pulsating "chandelier" configuration, as the reproductive
appendages become so engorged with fluid that the slugs'
bodies take on a "drained" appearance. It's such an ex-
hausting affair that the slugs are sure to eat the slimy rope
afterward to regain some of their spent energy.

*That's a lot to take in (for us and the slugs both), so if you need to take a cold
shower after all of that we'll understand.*

❯ "The Strange and
Sensational World of
Leopard Slug Sex,"
BBC, bbc.com; "Absurd
Creature of the Week:
This Slug Has Such a
Big Penis It Has to Mate
Upside Down," *Wired*,
wired.com

Paraponera clavata are called "bullet ants" because the pain from their sting is so intense that it's been likened to being shot with a gun. Another way the feeling has been described is "the worst pain known to man." For you or me, an encounter with a single bullet ant would probably mean a trip to the emergency room, followed by years of counseling. But the Sateré-Mawé tribe from Brazil will fill a glove full of them, and make their young warriors stick their hand inside to test their manhood.

> "The Worst Pain Known to Man . . . It's a Stinger," SciLogs, scilogs.com

That does sound pretty intense, and even more so if they sometimes mix up the words hand and manhood.

The only other insect able to deliver pain comparable to a bullet ant sting is an immense wasp called the tarantula hawk (genus *Hemipepsis*). The reason they were given that spectacular name is because when it's time to have babies, they actively begin hunting tarantulas, which are subdued, dragged underground, and paralyzed for the purpose of serving as an edible nursery for the wasp's larvae. But apart from that breathtaking horribleness, if one should ever have occasion to sink its stinger into a human, the ensuing agony is truly majestic. According to one testimonial, it's "like an electric wand that hits you, inducing an immediate, excruciating pain that simply shuts down one's ability to do anything, except, perhaps, scream."

> "Tarantula Hawk: Tarantula Hawk Stings Are the Most Painful of Any USA Insect," DesertUSA, desertusa.com

Treating physicians said they hadn't heard anything so terrifyingly dreadful since Paris Hilton's last studio album.

Sure, getting hit by a false tocandira ant (*Dinoponera gigantea*) will cause an inordinate amount of screaming in the short run, but eight hours later the pain will still be there, along with the additional party favors of cold sweats, nausea, and bloody stool. But honestly, if you do get stung you have no one to blame but yourself. Because there's no excuse for not noticing an ant that's upward of 2 goddamn inches long.

But maybe your brain didn't register that an ant could get that big, and you ignorantly reached down to comfort the poor, shiny black puppy with a bear trap for a face.

❯"Description of an Injury in a Human Caused by a False Tocandira (*Dinoponera gigantea*, Perty, 1833) with a Revision on Folkloric, Pharmacological and Clinical Aspects of the Giant Ants of the Genera *Paraponera* and *Dinoponera* (Subfamily Ponerinae)," by J.V. Haddad, J.L. Cardoso, and R.H. Moraes, *Revisto do Instituto de Medicina Tropical de São Paulo* (2005), ncbi.nlm.nih.gov

Puss caterpillars, the larvae of the southern flannel moth (*Megalopyge opercularis*), are colorfully cute, furry, and one of the most venomous creatures in the continental United States. They look like miniature Tribbles or something that might come as a toy in a Happy Meal, but underneath all that delightful fuzz is a minefield of toxic spines, just waiting to deliver you into a world of pain.

❯"Toxic 'Toupee': Explaining the Most Venomous Caterpillar in the U.S.," *National Geographic*, nationalgeographic.com

You know, this might very well point to a correlation between that thing Donald Trump wears on his head and why he's constantly grimacing.

If you visit the Arctic tundra at just the right time on the calendar, you can be bitten by mosquitoes 435 times in 5 minutes. If weather conditions are just right, various species such as the huge, slow-moving snow mosquito (*Aedes communis*), along with smaller, faster, and more vicious versions in the genus *Ochlerotatus*, can see their numbers explode to plague-level proportions. And according to anecdotal evidence, it's getting worse every year.

❯ "Bloodletting Worsens During Alaska's Legendary Mosquito Infestation," *Alaska Dispatch News*, adn.com

---

If you're wondering what being bitten 435 times in 5 minutes would look like (Would your body shrivel up like a deflated balloon? Would all those holes turn you into a blood-spraying lawn sprinkler?), the most logical answer is also pretty simple: Don't go to the Antarctic tundra under any circumstances whatsoever, and especially not during mosquito season, dumbass.

The Asian giant hornet (*Vespa mandarinia*) is the largest hornet in the world. They're as big as hummingbirds and decapitate honeybees as a part of their daily routine. Aside from their sheer incongruous humongous-ness, the venom in their stings is great for exploding red blood cells and causing kidney failure. And they got particularly aggressive in 2013, when they killed forty-two people and injured thousands in China. There's no confirmed word as of yet why they chose 2013 to go haywire and descend upon the populace, but the government has suggested that, until further notice, it might be a good idea to wear shirts with sleeves.

❯ "Deadly Giant Hornets Kill 42 People in China," CNN, cnn.com

And long pants, obviously. And a hockey mask. And a flamethrower if you can afford one.

You're probably aware that the reason fireflies put on their fabulous lightshow is for mating purposes. But not all of them have such a benign motive. *Photuris* fireflies imitate the signals that the females of other species use as a lovelight, but when an interested non-*Photuris* male responds to the sexy display, it is promptly dismembered and consumed.

I had a similar situation happen once in Tijuana. I guess I should be thankful that I only wound up with chronic gonorrhea.

> "Lured and Liquidated, Gullible Male Fireflies Supply 'Femmes Fatales' with a Lifesaving Chemical," *Cornell Chronicle*, cornell.edu

Some spiders expand their range by a process called "ballooning." It might sound like something fun, but remember, these are spiders we're talking about here. Anyway, right after baby spiders of certain species burst forth from their eggs, they will crawl up to the highest spot that's accessible, squirt out a strand of silk into the air, and let the wind carry them to parts unknown. That's all fine and good, except for those times when the sky becomes filled with tiny spiders, raining down fear from the heavens.

> "When Baby Spiders Rain Down from the Sky: Witness Describes Amazing Phenomenon," ABC News, abcnews. go.com

You'll know when incidents like this occur when the weatherman announcing the forecast is practically unintelligible due to the uncontrollable sobbing.

Spiders of the genus *Selenops* (called "flatties") have an aerodynamic body shape that not only lets them glide through the air but also allows them to control their pitch and yaw like they're piloting a hang glider. Or more accurately, like they're wearing a wingsuit. Researchers suspected that the flatties had this ability but felt they had to prove it by climbing to the top of the rainforest canopy and throwing spiders into the air like confetti.

What they didn't mention is how presumably drunk they were the night before, and how the guy in the tree totally lost a dare.

> "Arachnid Aloft: Directed Aerial Descent in Neotropical Canopy Spiders," by S.P. Yanoviak, Y. Munk, and R. Dudley, *Journal of the Royal Society Interface* (2015), rsif.royalsocietypublishing.org

---

Spiders have the ability to sail on the water as well as any salty seaman. Most of them are light enough that surface tension is their friend, allowing them to stay on top of the water instead of down where it's rather unpleasant. A variety of species take advantage of this talent by using their feet as rudders and silk as an improvised anchor. Some will even raise their legs in the air like a sail, and all of these abilities combined may be why spiders are able to distribute themselves so widely across the globe.

> "Spiders Can Sail Now, Which Is Terrifying," Public Radio International, pri.org

You really have to feel for the poor sailor whose ship has just sunk as he peers nervously into the water for sharks and then glances up for a second to see a goddamn spider staring him in the face.

Australian meat ants (*Iridomyrmex purpureus*) are about as pleasant as they sound, and farmers Down Under often employ them to clean up the dead, rotting animals on their property. To supplement their revolting diets, these ants have also developed a symbiotic relationship with a certain type of butterfly caterpillar. The caterpillar gets protection from predators, and in return the ants get to drink sugary fluids, fresh from a specialized organ in the vicinity of the caterpillar's ass.

It's not so different from herding cattle, really. The milking process is just a little more adult-themed.

❯ "Animal Species: Meat Ant," Australian Museum, australianmuseum.net.au

The "ant-mugging fly," *Milichia patrizii*, sneaks up on any ant foolish enough to separate itself from the herd and stuns it by violently grabbing its antennae. The mugger then forcefully extends its proboscis into the ant's mouth, compelling it to vomit up whatever food it may have been carrying back to the nest. The fly then gathers the puked-up meal and flies away, leaving the ant presumably shaken and forever scarred by such a blatant disregard for the rules of polite society.

In a few instances, victimized ants were observed immediately changing their political affiliations from liberal to conservative, and filling out applications to become brand-new members of the NRA.

❯ "Field Observations on *Milichia patrizii* Ant-Mugging Flies (Diptera: Milichiidae: Milichiinae) in KwaZulu-Natal, South Africa," by A.L. Wild and I. Brake, *African Invertebrates* (2009), bioone.org

Butterflies are wondrous and delicate creatures that would never knowingly cause harm to another living thing. Whoops! What I meant to say is that butterflies are dicks. In the Peruvian rainforest they will relentlessly harass turtles and then drink their sweet, delicious tears. The butterflies actually have a good reason for doing this (aside from the joys that come from behaving like unrepentant bullies). Because sodium can be scarce in the areas where they live, they will sometimes gang up on the turtles (and other creatures) in order to lick the salt from their tear ducts.

❯ "Why These Butterflies Are Drinking the Tears of a Turtle," BBC, bbc.com

---

I hate to think what they'd do to the poor turtles if they suddenly got a hankering for reptile milk.

Hungry frogs will often try to eat the larvae

of the *Epomis* ground beetle, which really isn't very surprising until you realize the frogs are actually the ones being hunted. In a case of gruesome role reversal, a grub will practically invite a frog to assault it. Then, when the frog fires out its sticky tongue, the grub will dodge nimbly to the side and latch on to its attacker's face or throat, "hanging on like a rodeo jockey." Eventually the frog tires out and the larva begins the process of eating it until only bones remain. And should a frog actually outmaneuver a grub and swallow it, that's no big deal. The grub simply starts devouring the frog from the inside.

❯ "Beetle Larva Lures and Kills Frogs, While the Adult Hunts and Paralyses Them," *Discover*, discovermagazine.com

Although I really don't think rodeos would be nearly as popular if the riders, after riding a bull for the required amount of time, were then given another eight seconds to wriggle down the animal's throat and burst out of its chest with a spleen in their teeth.

The sex life of the fruit fly known as *Drosophila bifurca* sounds like it must be a rather cumbersome affair for all parties involved. Mostly because the males have coiled sperm that's 20 times the length of its entire body. It the largest of its kind in nature, and for comparison it's 1,000 times as big as a human sperm. According to the source, if a 6-foot man had sperm like the fruit fly's it would rope out all the way to the 40-yard line of a football field.

❯"Longest Known Sperm Create Paradox of Nature," Live Science, livescience.com

Sure, that sounds incredibly gross, but if the New England Patriots were somehow able to incorporate it into a trick play, it could forever change the game as we know it.

The bombardier beetle (family Carabidae) was aptly named, for it possesses a very effective form of artillery-based weaponry: It can shoot hot chemicals out of its ass. The corrosive liquid they produce within their bodies is called benzoquinone, and the beetles are able to somehow superheat it and then violently explode it forth from their hindquarters. It works so well, practically nothing on the six continents in which they thrive will even attempt to eat them.

Not counting the patrons of various drinking establishments, where the substance has been repackaged and sold as something called "Old Milwaukee Lite."

❯"How Some Beetles Produce a Scalding Defensive Spray," Massachusetts Institute of Technology, mit.edu

South American *Odontomachus bauri* ants have formidable jaws that can snap shut in just 0.13 milliseconds and at a speed of 145 miles per hour. That's 100,000 times the force of gravity, and the fastest predatory strike among all animals. The snapping action is so powerful that they can aim their jaws at the ground and use the force to propel themselves into the air.

An ability that many of us wish we had in regard to threatening fingers, especially during annual prostate exams.

❯ "Ant Jaws Break Speed Record, Propel Insects into Air, Biologists Find," UC Berkeley News, berkeley.edu

❯ "Silent and Deadly: Fatal Farts Immobilize Prey," *Wired*, wired.com

The beaded lacewing (family Berothidae) is an elegant little flying insect, but at least one member species' larvae tend to be rather crude. The main food source for *Lomamyia latipennis* lacewings is termites, and to make sure their prey don't put up too much of a fight, the larvae first stun them with a "vapor-phase toxicant" that's released from their anuses. Yes, they fart on them.

Which is a strategy that's since been adopted by big brothers the world over.

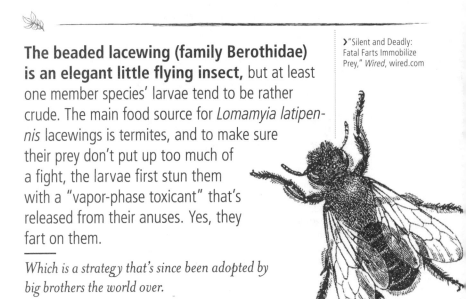

Some scientists believe that termite farts may produce as much as around 20 million tons of methane per year, which would be roughly 11 percent of all natural emissions on the planet. As a matter of fact, experts believe termite poots (and there may be as many as 250 trillion of them sounding off at any one time) just might be one of the major contributing factors involved in global warming.

Possibly ranking second only to the hot air produced by politicians and celebrities who complain about said global warming.

❯*Is It Hot in Here? The Simple Truth about Global Warming* by Nathan Todd Cool; "Global Warming? Blame It on Termite Farts," Metro DC Lawn and Garden Blog, mwcog.org

Velvet ants may look like congenial little balls of brightly colored fuzz, but in reality they're wasps. The females are wingless and could be mistaken for some sort of ant/muppet hybrid, but don't assume they're defenseless. Their sting is so horrendous that another nickname for them is "cow killer." Oh, and they also squeak when disturbed.

Sure, they might not be able to actually kill a cow, but they'll definitely do irreparable harm to any trust you might have in the toys your dog plays with.

❯"Beware the Squeak of the Cow Killer," *Washington Post*, washingtonpost.com

It seems that activities like building concealed underground web lairs and constructing trap doors are just the tip of the venom-filled iceberg where arachnid booby-trapping abilities are concerned. There's a South American species of ray spider (family Theridiosomatidae) that can turn its web into a slingshot. What they do is arrange their silk into the shape of a cone, rig it so that it's essentially spring-loaded, and then smash prey right out of the air with their improvised trebuchet.

To be fair, though, a quick death by massive blunt force trauma is about as merciful as spiders get.

❯"Crazy! Spider Launches Slingshot Web to Snag Prey," Live Science, livescience.com

The microscopic proto-arthropods known as tardigrades aren't insects exactly, but that's probably the closest description most people would recognize. They're cute in a freaky, chubby-alien-with-six-legs sort of way. Which explains why they're also called "water bears" or "moss piglets." They're also practically unkillable. They can be found in a wide range of areas, from the Himalayas to the bottom of the sea, and can survive in conditions that would be instantly fatal to just about any other creature on Earth. Experiments have shown that they're able to thrive and reproduce in outer space, and there's talk of sending them to colonize Mars.

Just further contributing to the distinct possibility that the movie Starship Troopers *will one day be viewed as a cautionary tale.*

> "Inside the Bizarre Genome of the World's Toughest Animal," *The Atlantic*, theatlantic.com

Ladybugs (also called ladybirds) are the farthest thing from cute. To begin with, they're red because they're poisonous to a variety of other animals. They also have babies that cannibalize each other, ooze toxic blood when annoyed, and brutally take the lives of around 5,000 innocent aphids during the course of their lifetimes. They're also usually riddled with mites, sexually promiscuous, and prone to STDs.

What "lady" did they name these bugs after? The women I normally hang around with have only three of those issues. Four, tops.

❯ "Pretty Ladybirds Are Disease-Ridden Cannibals," BBC, bbc.com

Harris's three-spot moths (*Harrisimemna trisignata*) have extraordinarily ugly caterpillars that are designed to look exactly like bird crap. As part of their disgusting disguise, they will save the discarded head capsules from previous molts, and then stick them to long white hairs poking out of their backs. Whenever they're startled, the caterpillars rattle the heads around, and there's a strong possibility they can use them as a bludgeoning weapon.

It's a pretty effective strategy really, because there's nothing scarier to a bird than haunted poop.

❯ *Owlet Caterpillars of Eastern North America* by David L. Wagner, Dale F. Schweitzer, J. Bolling Sullivan, and Richard C. Reardon

The velvet worm (*Onychophora*) is slow and blind and hasn't changed much at all in the past 500 million years. This could lead the uninitiated to think these creatures are practically defenseless. Until you come to find their Latin name means "claw bearers," and that they're able to unleash what is essentially a slime cannon. Velvet worms are able to fire strands of glue at prey up to a foot away, completely immobilizing the unwary. Then all that's left to do is lumber up and end their misery with a set of nasty, unseen jaws.

> "Animal Species: Velvet Worm," Australian Museum, australianmuseum.net.au

It's merely coincidence that "The Velvet Worm" also happened to be my stage name back in my dancing days. But let's not dwell on that.

A few years ago an arachnid was observed in the Peruvian Amazon doing something so strange that science still hasn't recovered enough to give it a common name.

It appears to be a species of orb weaver, and what it does is use its silk to create a believable doppelgänger of itself in the middle of its web. Indeed, they are building scarecrows. As yet it's unknown what exactly they're up to with this gambit. In addition to using their own silk, the spiders will include leaves and other plant debris, along with the body parts of dead insects they have killed.

> "Spider That Builds Its Own Spider Decoys Discovered," *Wired*, wired.com

It's hard to believe that a spider could actually be practicing witchcraft, but . . . well . . . no, I guess it's not.

San Jose, California, is the flashpoint for war.
An ant war, that is. The invasive Argentine ant (*Linepithema humile*) has established a beachhead and is waging furious battles with the local ant species for control of not just the nerd mecca but also possibly the entire southwestern United States. From all accounts, they appear to be winning. Handily. The best evidence for this is the fact that they've established a "mega colony," one that includes a series of underground, interconnected, and cooperative nests that spans 560 miles.

The possibility exists that thousands of individual ants have already merged together, Voltron-style, and have been appearing in public for years under the assumed name of "Mel Gibson." Which would explain a lot of things.

❯ "In San Jose, an Epic Battle of the Ants," *The Mercury News,* mercurynews.com

A newly described species of mosquito was found to have evolved specifically to live in the London subway system. *Culex molestus* (named for their love of molesting people) got their start during World War II, when a few members of a mosquito species that specialized in birds found a more captive audience underground and began feasting on the thousands of people taking shelter from the German Blitz. Eventually they became a species unto themselves, and continue to torment Tube riders to this very day.

❯ "The Unique Mosquito That Lives in the London Underground," BBC, bbc.com

Getting bitten by mosquitoes on the subway sounds annoying, but really, anything that might cut down on the percentage of public masturbators should be viewed as a positive.

Huntsman spiders (family Sparassidae) in Australia

Huntsman spiders (family Sparassidae) in Australia can be as large as a dinner plate and are to arachnophobes what Hitler was to European political stability. They're actually considered pretty harmless, however, as they fit squarely into the old "more afraid of you than you are of it" category. But while you're unlikely to be bitten by a huntsman spider under normal circumstances, they can be absolutely lethal in another, rather unexpected way: vehicular manslaughter. Which makes more sense when you learn that it's not uncommon for these expansive arachnids to seek shelter in cars, especially under the sun visors, and leap out suddenly when the car is in motion.

> ❯ "Gallery: 10 Most Dangerous Spiders in Australia," *Australian Geographic,* australiangeographic.com.au

So now when you visit Australia and rent a car, you'll understand what the unusual surcharge in the contract that reads "sudden death by waking nightmare insurance" is all about.

Tawny crazy ants (*Nylanderia fulva,*) so named for the spastic way they move

Tawny crazy ants (*Nylanderia fulva,*) so named for the spastic way they move around, are rather scrawny even as ants go. But what they lack in size they more than make up for with an absurd ability to multiply. Originally from South America, they've successfully invaded the Southeast United States, where they now outnumber every other species of ant 100–1 in some areas of Texas. But what they seem to love even more than reproducing is electronics. That is, swarming *inside* electronics. Crazy ants will invade things like computers, air conditioning units and pretty much anything that runs on electricity. And should they get fried in there, that just makes them emit a smell that attracts more crazy ants.

> ❯ "The Rise of the Crazy Ants," *Scientific American,* scientificamerican.com; "Why 'Crazy Ants' Swarm Inside Electronics," Live Science, livescience.com

Meanwhile, members of the Texas Best Buy "Geek Squad" are training furiously with 5-pound weights to face the greatest challenge of their lives.

CHAPTER 5

Menacing Mammal Maliciousness

When asked what the most dangerous animal on Earth is, the insufferably smug person in the room will invariably say, "man." First of all, that's sexist. And furthermore, that person has clearly never exited a shower to find a band of startled raccoons. Yes, humans can be gross, but nobody I've ever met can poop forty times in one day like a panda and survive. Just because something's fuzzy and warm does not preclude a cold heart. Mammals can go to war, commit cruel and unusual deeds, and become addicted to porn just like that uncle nobody likes getting into conversations with at family reunions. And if you think you're somehow superior to all the other lowly beasts that skitter, slither, or squirm just because you belong to the vaunted class Mammalia, or somehow entitled because you're a card-carrying member of the order Primate, see how proud you feel after learning that . . .

Primates don't come much stupider-looking than male proboscis monkeys, whose oversized noses (used for amplifying the volume of their annoying honks) hang down well past their mouths. But as dopey as they look, the face might not be the physical feature that burns itself into your memory after an encounter. Because they also have bright red, permanently erect penises that are so off-putting that the monkeys sometimes use them to intimidate foes.

> "The Amazing Swimming Proboscis Monkey (Part I)," *Scientific American*, scientificamerican.com

Proboscis monkeys can live for up to twenty years in the wild, and possibly thirty if they swallow their pride and visit an urologist.

Prairie dogs sure are cute. The adorable way they pop their heads out of their burrows and look around has made their colonies a tourist attraction in places like Utah and South Dakota. What's not so endearing is how prairie dogs routinely murder baby squirrels by chasing them down and shaking them to death. This behavior is the first recorded instance of serial herbivorous-mammal-on-herbivorous-mammal homicide, and it basically comes down to a turf war, occurring when both species are competing for the same real estate and food.

> "Biologists Have Learned Something Horrifying about Prairie Dogs," Gizmodo, gizmodo.com

If you find this information too disturbing, you could always visit the closest Chuck E. Cheese's and exact some imaginary justice at the whack-a-mole game.

Despite what your childhood trips to the water park might have led you to believe, seals aren't all about flipper clapping and handstands. They're carnivores, after all, and so a certain level of violence is simply an unavoidable aspect of their nature. But what's a little harder to accept is some species' propensity for completely unnecessary assaults on other animals, for purposes that have nothing to do with food whatsoever. All right, I'll stop beating around the bush—Antarctic fur seals are raping penguins, and scientists have no idea why.

———

Some suggested it might have something to do with the penguins' shape and color patterns, until Facebook accusations of "victim shaming" compelled them to immediately check their privilege and attend lengthy sensitivity training.

❯"Multiple Occurrences of King Penguin (*Aptenodytes patagonicus*) Sexual Harassment by Antarctic Fur Seals (*Arctocephalus gazella*)," by W.A. Haddad, R.R. Reisinger, T. Scott, M.N. Bester, and P.J.N. de Bruyn, *Polar Biology* (2015), link. springer.com

While European settlers often take the blame for introducing lots of diseases to the Native American population all those years ago, tuberculosis may not have been one of them. Because, according to recent research, seals did it.

———

The theory hasn't been confirmed yet, but some have suggested we enact a law that requires each and every seal on Earth to wear one of those surgical facemasks, along with a cute little T-shirt with the word UNCLEAN on the back.

❯"Seals Brought TB to Americas," *Nature*, nature.com

In 1999 a murder investigation was launched in a South African game park after a number of white rhinos were found dead. Their ivory was intact, so it probably wasn't poachers. It seems they may have been indirectly involved in the crime, however, as it was revealed that the culprits were a gang of juvenile elephants that had grown up orphaned due to ivory hunters. But even pachyderms that don't come from broken homes will sometimes violently turn on their fellow beasts, like the time a photographer watched in horror as a female ran a Cape buffalo through with one of her tusks, simply because the buffalo looked at her funny.

According to the dictionary, the correct term is herd or parade. But maybe we should start calling these groups of elephants "MS-13s."

> "The Delinquents: A Spate of Rhino Killings," CBS News, cbsnews.com; "Bizarre Photographs of an Elephant Attacking and Killing a Resting Buffalo," Rhino Africa, rhinoafrica.com

Common chimpanzees (*Pan troglodytes*) are our closest living relatives, and delight young and old alike with their playful antics. That is, when they're not engaging in coordinated, sustained battles against their own kind. Just as humans are unfortunately prone to frequent wars amongst themselves, so too will chimps happily slaughter their neighbors in order to pillage the spoils of the conquered. The tactics generally employed include ganging up on an enemy male, and then ripping his ears and testes off before committing the deathblow. The aggressors then proceed to beat up the females and cannibalize the babies.

> "Chimps Engage in 'War' for Turf," Seeker, seeker.com

"Chimp-Conan, what is best in life?" "To crush your enemies, to see them driven before you, and to hear the lamentation of their women. Also a shitload of bananas."

While chimps are prone to havoc and wanton violence, a related primate species called bonobos (*Pan paniscus*) prefers to settle their differences in quite a different manner: hot ape sex. Their motto seems to be "Let's all have a jungle orgy, not war." And although they can develop feelings for individual members of the opposite sex, there is no judgment should their partners spread their hairy love around. This promiscuity seems to work out well for the bonobos, because if you offer a group of them a pile of food, they'll all squish their filthy ape genitals together to help decide how to divvy it all up.

❯"7 Things Bonobos Can Teach Us about Love and Sex," *Psychology Today*, psychologytoday.com

Wrinkle up your face in disgust if you must, but it's little different than how your great-grandmother probably made it through the Depression.

A troublingly human-like quality has also been observed in baboons: mass hysteria. We can't confirm yet whether this behavior occurs in the wild, but in 2013 the troop of hamadryas baboons (*Papio hamadryas*) kept at Emmen Zoo in the Netherlands suddenly began acting . . . off. The normally spastic simians began moping around listlessly and refused to eat, as if every one of them had just experienced some sort of psychological trauma. It was like they had collectively gone on strike against the Playful Antics Union, and theories as to why ranged from ghosts to UFOs to the possibility that somebody had walked by wearing a T-shirt with a lion graphic.

Yeah, the only way theories like that come from "experts" is if they're the kind that read the bumps on your head at the carnival.

❯"Spooked Baboons Baffle Dutch Zoo in Emmen," BBC News, bbc.com

Naked mole-rats (*Heterocephalus glaber*) are indeed quite nude. They're also immune to pain (no receptors in their skin) and can chew straight through a cinderblock with those industrial chisels they call teeth. That's enough for a straight-to-video Kevin Bacon vehicle right there. But the most disconcerting thing about these rancorous rodents is how they exhibit insect hive behavior. Researchers are still trying to figure out what the hell is going on exactly, but naked mole-rat colonies have one queen (like wasps). She's the only female capable of breeding, and she grows more corpulent than any of her subjects (like bees), which are all assigned very specific tasks to perform for the remainder of their lives (like ants).

Clearly it's only a– matter of time until the cackling supervillain responsible for this madness makes his existence known. Somebody better expose himself to gamma rays or get bitten by a radioactive spider like yesterday.

❯"Scientists Amazed by the Mole Rat's Bizarre Behavior," *New York Times,* nytimes.com; "Mammals—Naked Mole-Rat," San Diego Zoo, sandiegozoo.org

There aren't many rodents lucky enough to have names as magnificent as the Thor's hero shrew (*Scutisorex thori*), and fewer still that deserve it as much as they do. The reason these shrews are so heroic is that they have evolved a bizarre, fortified spine that might be sturdier than any other vertebrate's. A fully grown man can stand directly on top of one of them (or even tie them to his feet and wear them like shoes) and they'll suffer no ill effects whatsoever.

❯"New Species, Thor's Hero Shrew, Will Back Itself in Any Feat of Strength," *Scientific American,* scientificamerican.com; "Hero Shrew Found, One of 'Most Bizarre Animals on Earth,'" *National Geographic,* nationalgeographic.com

Which is all very impressive, but for gardening enthusiasts it just means that if they want their tomatoes to survive, they're going to have to spend a fortune on sledgehammers.

***Daubentonia madagascariensis*, or the aye-aye, is a creature** you may have already seen images of on the Internet—possibly because they're so disturbing to look at that it's become a popular way to frighten grandmothers via e-mail. The aye-aye is a primate, or more specifically, the world's ugliest lemur. They come from the madman's menagerie that is Madagascar, and are nocturnal, as befits an animal with the appearance of hell spawn. They spend most of their lives in trees (when they're not raiding coconut plantations and scarring children's psyches), creeping out every other animal in the jungle that happens to look up. It's there that they use their disconcertingly long, skeletal middle fingers to "tap" on the trunks of trees to locate and dig out vermin to devour.

❯ "Aye-Aye (*Daubentonia madagascariensis*)," Duke Lemur Center, lemur. duke.edu

If you think I'm being too hard on aye-ayes and that "even ugly animals need love too," I'd suggest taking a good hard look at one. Yes, I'm glad you agree. There is a limit.

On a list of the least frightening animals on Earth, most people would put deer right at the top (unless they've recently had one as an unwelcome guest through a front windshield). But something those lists don't account for is "vampire deer." I'm not screwing around here—there are actually a few species of Bambi that have fangs as intimidating as any extinct saber-tooth. The Asian water deer (*Hydropotes inermis*) is one, and the Himalayan musk deer (family Moschidae) is another. There's even one that just reappeared, sixty years after the last confirmed sighting. None of these deer use their oversized canines to suck the blood of the living, thankfully, as they're actually used for territorial and mating disputes.

❯ "Rare Deer with Fangs Is Spotted for First Time in 60 Years," *Telegraph*, telegraph.co.uk

Nonetheless, should you ever come across a petting zoo with the word vampire anywhere in the title, you should definitely keep driving.

When they see a creature as furry and cute as a koala (*Phascolarctos cinereus*), most people's first inclination is to cuddle it, along with perhaps some light nuzzling. Unfortunately, that decision would be rather ill-advised, since around 90 percent of the koala population in certain parts of Australia has chlamydia. An inordinate number of them also have the marsupial version of HIV.

So that's why you don't see that Qantas Airways mascot anymore. Because it's hard to attract customers when your company spokesman is riddled with STDs.

❯"Dual Epidemics Threaten Koalas," NOVA, pbs.org

After a period of breastfeeding on mother's milk, it's time for koala "joeys" to start eating the eucalyptus leaves that will sustain them for the rest of their lives. Unfortunately, they're still too young to properly process the hard-to-digest plant material. So the next stage in the nursing process is to suckle on specialized feces, straight from Mom's butthole.

Dr. Oz hasn't gone on Oprah to promote this yet, so new mothers might want to jump on the bandwagon quick to get the maximum amount of hipness points out of this hot new trend.

❯"Life Cycle of the Koala," Australian Koala Foundation, savethekoala.com

European badgers (*Meles meles*) are pretty tough customers, and interactions with them can be so hazardous that the Germans felt they had to create a specific breed of dog (the wienery dachshund) to deal with their claw-wielding feistiness. The British might want to consider taking a similar measure soon, seeing as how the citizenry (both past and present) have been having a peculiar issue with them over the past few years. Namely, badgers are digging up human graves and pulling out the bones to feast upon.

❯ "Council Powerless to Stop Grave-Disturbing Badgers in Swindon," BBC News, bbc.co.uk

Besides, those stuffy dog shows could use something like a "Grave Robber Death Hound" to spice up the proceedings.

As expected, I suppose, elephants have massive penises to go along with their massive everything else. What's surprising is that pachyderm dongs are so gargantuan that they're often mistaken for fifth legs. They're also prehensile, and can even be used to scratch an itch, swat away flies, and issue a very personal warning to overzealous tourists.

Many an elephant rampage might have been prevented if only a careless zookeeper hadn't accidentally and too-vigorously scrubbed the wrong appendage.

❯ "South African Wildlife—Wait, That's Not a Trunk . . .," *Discover*, discovermagazine.com

Elephants are apparently violent drunks. While the rumor that they love to get sauced in the wild by eating fermented fruit has been proven to be a myth, it does seem to be true that Asian elephants will occasionally trample and rampage through Indian villages to steal liquor. Which, of course, only makes them rampage harder.

And one would imagine their fury is only magnified in the mornings, when they wake up in the middle of a herd of ugly but satisfied cattle.

❯ "Is Every Single Elephant a Village-Wrecking Booze Hound?" Live Science, livescience.com

America has its own large mammals that happen to be substance-abusing degenerates: bighorn sheep. Their drug of choice is a mind-altering lichen, and in order to procure it the sheep will gladly clamber across sheer cliff faces, risking both life and limb in the process. And some sheep get so desperate for a fix that they'll gnaw at rocks until their teeth are worn down to the gums.

Just in case you wondered what the deal was with those sheep in G–strings offering sexual favors behind the Greyhound station.

❯ *Intoxication: The Universal Drive for Mind-Altering Substances* by Ronald K. Siegel, PhD

Giant anteaters (*Myrmecophaga tridactyla*) normally don't get a whole lot of respect. The reason being, well, just look at them. Probably close to the last thing most people worry about when in the presence of these long-nosed, bushy-tailed freaks is the potential for getting disemboweled. But it should be right at the very top. Because the same fearsome claws that anteaters use to tear apart termite mounds are just as good for slaughtering entire flocks of flamingos when they get the inclination (as evidenced during an unfortunate incident at a Swedish zoo in 2011). And they have a proven track record of butchering hunters and zookeepers who made the fatal mistake of not giving them the credit they deserve.

❯ "Giant Anteaters Can Kill People," Live Science, livescience.com; "Anteater Kills Flock of Flamingoes," UPI, upi.com

You wouldn't imagine that something could ever be that scary when it doesn't even have a single tooth in its mouth. Well, unless you take into account the fact that Tommy Lee Jones and Clint Eastwood are probably wearing dentures at this point.

When veggies and fruit are scarce, Sumatran orangutans (*Pongo abelii*) will sometimes change teams from herbivore to carnivore. And since these great apes aren't exactly the most proficient hunters, they will target one of the easiest animals in the forest to catch: the unsuspecting and impossibly cute slow loris (look it up if you want to spend the next hour crying). The orangutans seem to be a little fussy about how they go about consuming their smaller fellow primates: They start by sucking out the brains and then follow up by gnawing off the genitals.

❯ "Vegetarian Orangutans Eat World's Cutest Animal," *New Scientist*, newscientist.com; "Meat-Eating by Adult Female Sumatran Orangutans (*Pongo pygmaeus abelii*)," by S.S. Utami and J.A.R.A.M. van Hooff, *American Journal of Primatology* (1997), sumatranorangutan.org

This is surely news that the conservation folks would prefer to keep under wraps. It would be like if a panda was caught on tape offering candy to an underage white rhino to lure it into a van.

Way back when, around 150 years ago or so, a number of common house mice (*Mus musculus*) found themselves on remote Gough Island in the South Atlantic after jumping ship from European sailing vessels. Gough Island is known as an important breeding colony for seabirds, whose chicks happen to be just about the only edible things around. You can probably see where this is going. So the mice adapted their behavior from "opportunistic scavenger" to "serial killer" practically overnight, and began gnawing away on live seabird chicks with reckless abandon. It's now estimated that the Gough Island mice are murdering millions of baby birds every year.

If the Gilligan's Island gang had landed on that particular island, it would have been a very different show indeed. Most episodes would probably have centered around the Professor trying to cure Gilligan's and everyone else's PTSD.

❯ "Giant Killer Mice Decimating Rare Seabirds," *National Geographic*, nationalgeographic.com

As anyone who's seen *Napoleon Dynamite* knows, when a daddy lion and a mama tiger love each other very much, something called a liger can be born. What you may not be aware of is that the coupling of these two species can sometimes produce animals of ridiculously massive proportions. We're talking 1,000 pounds of cat-beast here. And they're also fast. Apparently ligers can run at 60 mph, which would make them second only to the cheetah in terms of sprinting ability. Conversely, the tigon (which is what happens when a male tiger and a female lion get drunk at an office party) is much scrawnier than either of the parents.

❯ "Why Ligers Are Bigger Than Tigons," Ligers.org; "Speed of the Ligers," Liger World, ligerworld.com

So if you've ever had reservations about leaving your Great Dane and Chihuahua alone in the same room overnight, you should definitely follow your instincts. The world doesn't need any more abominations.

In a controlled study at Duke University Medical Center, monkeys were found to enjoy (and be willing to pay for) pornography. The study went like this: Twelve adult male rhesus macaques (*Macaca mulatta*) were shown "sexy photographs" (let's not dwell on what that could entail) of lady monkeys, and were rewarded with juice whenever they moved on to a different picture (one that wasn't of a primate in a wet T-shirt or whatever). What they found was that the macaques were willing to forego their juice, and even give up the juice they had already earned, in order to bring back the images of hot, hot monkey-porn.

> ❯ "Monkeys Like Porn Too," ABC Science, abc.net.au

Perhaps the most important thing to take away from all this is that if you have children who are interested in pursuing a career in science, you should probably steer them away from Duke.

The Australian, mouse-like creatures known as *Antechinus* aren't rodents but marsupials. But they have a sex life that would scandalize the randiest rat. Every year during *Antechinus* mating season, the males engage in so much frenzied humping that the stress of it all kills them. This works out just great for the females, since with half the population gone, they and their young have lots more to eat.

So depending on how you look at it, if you ever happen upon a group of women at a bar who all have Antechinus *tattoos, you should be either very excited or very afraid.*

❯ "These Newly Discovered Marsupials Basically Sex Each Other to Death," *Washington Post*, washingtonpost.com

The yellow-bellied marmots (*Marmota flaviventris*) in California's Sequoia National Park are inquisitive little creatures. And by that I mean they're a huge pain in the ass. In 2002 they were wreaking havoc all over the park, chewing through the brake lines and radiator hoses on cars. Why? It's believed that they were doing this to get high on antifreeze.

❯"Is That a Marmot Under My Hood?" National Wildlife Federation, nwf.org

This presumably led the park rangers to fear for the local toad population, which was still recovering from the onslaught of local college students who had nearly licked them to extinction.

The mating ritual of goats can be considered a very intimate and romantic affair, if you happen to be a degenerate pervert. In order to advertise his willingness to mount a member of the opposite sex, a male goat will begin by urinating all over himself in order to get his hormones wafting around in the air. He will then approach a female goat and determine her availability by letting her urinate all over his face. This will cause the male to "run his tongue in and out of his mouth," become "generally very excited," and produce a noise that sounds like "Wup! Wup! Wup!"

And in case you were wondering what happens next, it should be pretty obvious. Spoiler: it's lots of pissy goat sex.

❯"Behavioral and Mating Habits of Goats," Onion Creek Ranch, tennesseemeatgoats.com; "Behavior," Goat Handbook, goatworld.com; "Goat Behavior, Characteristics and FYI," Fias Co Farm, fiascofarm.com

Mountain goats (*Oreamnos americanus*) don't just love the smell and taste of their own foul effluent, they like human pee as well. They might even like it more. These sure-footed sociopaths are notorious for frenziedly licking up the spots where hikers have recently relieved themselves, and warnings need to be posted to keep people from pissing on trails. Because an angry goat could very easily kill a human, and especially, presumably, when there's one around that won't comply with its depraved needs.

So if you're ever lost in the wilderness, you could try peeing like you've never peed before, and maybe a goat will show up to lead you to safety. Or maybe it'll just force you to perform certain . . . activities . . . while it watches.

❯ "Don't Pee on That Trail," *Outside*, outsideonline.com

Male Barbary macaques (*Macaca sylvanus*) are creatures with very specific . . . needs. Apparently when these monkeys have sex, they cannot reach orgasm unless the female screams. Why this is the case has been a subject of much debate among primatologists, and various studies were conducted in which the monkeys' vigorous pelvic thrusts were closely scrutinized. There are no conclusive answers as of yet, but surely the scientists will continue staring at monkeys screwing until they can come up with a definite answer to this vexing question.

❯ "Study Reveals Why Monkeys Shout During Sex," Live Science, livescience.com

Over and over. As long as necessary. Sometimes during the weekends, with friends and a cooler full of beer.

Sloths (families Megalonychidae and Bradypodidae) are so torpid that algae grow on them—which they eat, of course. And they're so incredibly useless that watching one cross a road is like watching a drunk navigate through glue. It's such a pathetic sight that motorists in Ecuador (those who don't obliterate them under their tires, at least) are sometimes compelled to ask for police assistance in helping get their sorry asses across. Why do they even come out of the trees in the first place? Well, their bowels are slow too, and every seven days they need to come down to crap.

And considering it probably takes forever for them to do that, one would imagine the roads in Ecuador are a serious mess on a number of levels.

❯ "Sloth Mystery Solved: How Moths and Algae Shape This Unusual Creature's Toilet Habits," *Independent*, independent .co.uk; "Officer Helps Sloth Cross the Road," CNN, cnn.com

Sloths have been recorded no fewer than twenty-five times sneaking (something they might actually be good at) into human settlements under cover of night and raiding the outdoor latrines. That's right, they were eating human poop! Experts believed they must be obtaining some sort of nutritional benefit from these midnight toilet raids, but it was "unclear exactly what that might be."

❯ "Sloths' Bizarre 'Toilet Habit' Recorded in Amazon, Peru," BBC, bbc.co.uk

Yes, it is indeed confusing how an animal that snacks on slimy fungus that grows on its ass could ever put raw sewage in its mouth.

The crested rat (*Lophiomys imhausi*) of South Africa looks like some weird version of a porcupine, but it's most definitely a rat. A poison rat. Oh, it's not poisonous all on its own. What the crested rat does is chew the bark of a highly toxic tree into a goop, and then spreads it all over its back until it's all sopped up by specially absorbent hairs. Then ta da! The rat is now equipped with a noxious Mohawk that will give any creature ignorant enough to attack it a bad case of the deads.

❯ "Spiky Rat Applies Plant Poison to Turn Hair Deadly," *National Geographic*, nationalgeographic.com

The careless overuse of dangerously powerful hair-care products may also explain the sudden disappearance of many bands from the 1980s. Some still speak of this terrifying phenomenon, in hushed whispers, as the "Flock of Seagulls Effect."

The African antelopes known as topis (*Damaliscus lunatis*) travel in herds across the savannah and occasionally cross paths with other herds during their journey. And sometimes a female within one of the herds might look wistfully over to a male from another, and attempt to saunter off and into the arms of a competitor. As a countermeasure to her wandering eye, the dominant male from her own group will make the same panicked call that topis usually use to announce the presence of a hungry lion, thereby scaring the crap out of the female and keeping her on the straight and narrow.

❯ "Sexual Deception Spotted Among Antelopes," *USA Today*, usatoday.com

And that's why whenever I go with my daughter to the mall, the first thing I do is pull the fire alarm. She then has precisely ten minutes to complete her shopping.

The African spiny mouse has an incredible ability to regenerate tissue. This skill comes in very handy for this particular rodent, because they way spiny mice escape from predators is that they "jettison strips of skin from their own hides" when threatened. And sometimes that means they'll discard 60 percent of the skin on their backs, while the horrifying sight that remains scurries off to find shelter.

One would imagine that this behavior would cause any normal cat to discontinue further pursuit, and immediately contact its therapist to see if there is an opening for an emergency session.

❯ "Spiny Mice Defend Themselves with Self-flaying Skin and Fast Healing Factors," *National Geographic*, nationalgeographic.com

Many animals we think of as strict herbivores aren't averse to deviating from their vegetarian lifestyle now and again. Deer, sheep, giraffes, and other plant-nibbling species will occasionally chomp down a small, live animal (or pieces of a dead one). Whether it's to alleviate a calcium deficiency or simply due to straight-up meanness, cows are even known to gobble down baby chicks whole. And a cow in India named Lal gleefully mangled forty-eight chickens in a month.

❯ "This Poor Chicken Got Eaten by a Cow," *Smithsonian*, smithsonianmag.com

I have to say, if they were feeding those chickens bacon, this whole scenario sounds absolutely delicious.

Not only are giant pandas (*Ailuropoda melano-leuca*) so useless at mating that it's a major news event whenever one gives birth, the babies they do produce are repulsive, hairless, and about the size of a gerbil. Cementing their utter failure at what one might suppose would be the relatively simple task of propagating their own goddamn species, panda mothers often accidentally crush their infants under the weight of their fat, lazy, adorable asses. Some breeding programs have even resorted to showing pandas bear-on-bear pornography to get them in the mood.

———

Which must be very exciting news for those who enjoy dressing up like My Little Pony characters and calling themselves things like "Twinklewhisper" online.

❯ "Try Not to Get Too Excited about the Rare Birth of Panda Triplets," *Washington Post*, washingtonpost.com; "'Panda Porn' to Boost Male's Sex Drive," ABC News, abcnews.com

Sea otters (*Enhydra lutris*) are famous for charming onlookers with their antics as they whack clams on their bellies with rocks. But one such antic that doesn't get a lot of press is their habit of raping baby seals, and sometimes killing them in the process. And they're not especially bothered when that happens, because they'll just keep on having sex with that dead baby seal. For days.

❯ "The Other Side of Otters," Seeker, seeker.com

———

So that's why some people call them "the clowns of the sea." Because of all the rape murders.

Giant river otters are also known as "river wolves" because they live in packs and communicate via howling. They can reach 6 feet long and are perfectly capable of murdering caimans (the toothier, South American version of crocodiles). Piranhas and anacondas are also on the menu, which suggests a lack of fear—and that humans would be wise to give them a wide berth. An especially ominous sign comes from reports of how they like to "tease wildlife videographers and then swim away laughing."

❯"7 Surprising Facts about the Giant River Otter," *National Geographic*, nationalgeographic.com

Yes, it's all very cute until someone eventually catches them acting like their ocean relatives, gleefully raping a capybara.

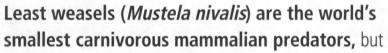

Least weasels (*Mustela nivalis*) are the world's smallest carnivorous mammalian predators, but they might be one of the most ferocious. They sure are cute, though. Which makes it rather disconcerting to happen upon one engaging in its favorite hobby: bloodthirsty killing sprees. Least weasels are able to kill prey five times their size, and the way they do it is by latching themselves on to a victim's neck and just hanging there, draining blood out of the jugular vein. Once the prey is sufficiently deceased, the first thing the weasels eat is the brain.

It's hard to reconcile something so adorable engaging in such brutal acts. It's kind of like that old Full House *episode where one of the Olsen twins stabbed a hobo.*

❯"Cute Little Killers," *St. Albert Gazette*, stalbertgazette.com; *The Biology of Small Mammals* by Joseph F. Merritt

If you had to guess which large animal is responsible for the most violent deaths in Africa, which animal would you suppose that would be? Hint: it's not lions or crocodiles. Give up? It's goddamn hippos. Not only are these easily pissed-off mega-mammals able to run faster than the fleetest Olympian sprinter in short bursts, their immense tusks and incisors are great for snapping boats, and the humans within them, completely in half.

❯"Up Close and Personal with the Hippos of Uganda," ABC News, abcnews.go.com

I guess we should have known that all the fat shaming would come back to haunt us eventually.

Apart from the whole savage impalement thing,

hippos are a pleasure to watch as they lumber about in their comical, yet somehow majestic way. Except for when they're spinning their tails like propellers to spray their feces around. That unsightly display is actually how hippos communicate, and it's a ritual of sorts. Dominant males will splatter subordinates to remind them who's in charge, and the subordinates might return the favor to signal their obedience. And of course the mating procedure is just a complete shit-show as well.

Which is probably a big part of the reason zoos don't have hippo shows like they do with dolphins. The splash zone wouldn't be nearly as fun, and every audience member would have to get a hepatitis shot before she left the park.

❯"Hippopotamus, *Hippopotamus amphibius*, and Pygmy Hippopotamus, *Choeropsis liberiensis*," San Diego Zoo, sandiegozoo.org

Not far down on the disagreeable list are the African or Cape buffalo (*Syncerus caffer*). A popular nickname for these 1,300-pound slabs of orneriness is "black death," which they earned by killing more big-game hunters than any other African beast. Another catchy one is "widow-maker." With their curved horns that come together in the middle to form a battering ram and unreasonably surly dispositions, even if you're not a hunter trying to shoot them in the face there's little chance of talking your way out of a fatal goring once they've chosen you for culling.

Many of the fatalities may have been the result of the cruel but popular initiation prank that veteran hunters often play on the new guy: "Go up and milk that bull."

> "Unusual African Buffalo Facts: Why Are They So Feared by Hunters?" Africa Wildlife Detective, africa-wildlife-detective.com

The striped polecat (*Ictonyx striatus*) looks something like a skunk, but it's more like a giant weasel. And the stink it can produce is far more putrid than anything Pepé le Pew ever jettisoned from his sphincter. This polecat's secretions are legendary for their olfactory odiousness, and the chemical cocktail that exudes from its glands is so powerfully rank that it allows a creature the size of a household tabby to face down an entire pride of lions.

The skunks, having learned that they aren't the world champions of stank after all, have been rumored to be upping their game with a strict new diet of asparagus and chalupas.

> "Striped Polecat," Kruger National Park, krugerpark.co.za

Hyenas are rather unsavory creatures, and it's no accident that they're often the villains in talking-animal cartoons. And their cubs appear to be chips off the old chopping block. If there's a runt born into a hyena litter, the bigger cubs will savagely bully it, often to death. And sometimes the weaker sibling receives so much abuse that it may seek shelter in an underground hiding place, and remain there in abject terror until it eventually starves.

Not for nothing, but has anyone really looked into why Octomom's reality show got canceled all of a sudden?

❯ "Siblicide in the Spotted Hyena: Analysis with Ultrasonic Examination of Wild and Captive Individuals," by S.A. Wahaj, N.J. Place, M.L. Weldele, S.E. Glickman, and K.E. Holekamp, *Behavioral Ecology* (2007), beheco.oxfordjournals.org

❯ "Margay," International Society for Endangered Cats (ISEC) Canada, wildcatconservation.org

The margay (*Leopardus wiedii*), a small Central and South American jungle cat, has learned to do an impression of a baby pied tamarin monkey (*Saguinus bicolor*) in distress. The cat's favorite way to perform this trick is while hidden in some bushes in the vicinity of those aforementioned primates. And when Mama or Papa Monkey comes over to see what manner of trouble Junior has gotten into this time, the margay will pounce in an attempt to devour them.

At which time the cat breaks into its other favorite impression: Arnold Schwarzenegger one-liners. You know, stuff like "Hasta la vista, monkey," and "Get to the choppa! The one that's in my mouth!" It's really annoying.

For a while it was believed that when mountain gorillas (*Gorilla beringei graueri*) in Rwanda ate too much bamboo at a certain time of year, the plant material would ferment in their stomachs and have the effect of getting them roaring drunk. And it seemed they could be angry drunks, as supported by an incident wherein a wildlife photographer got a little too close to an apparently-inebriated male and got himself punched right in his stupid face. But as it turns out, gorilla stomachs don't work that way, and the gorillas weren't drunk after all. The more likely explanation is that they were right in the middle of a sugar high.

> "Can a Gorilla Really Get Drunk from Bamboo?" *Smithsonian*, smithsonianmag.com

If they had just asked any parent who bought the wrong type of cereal for their toddlers, all this confusion could have been avoided.

Wombats poop cubes. You heard right, cubes.

How precisely they manage to produce a six-sided, box-like turd from their ass is a subject that nobody wants to dwell on, but you probably want to know why. The reason for the angular, non-rolling shape is so that the wombats can place their feces out in the open on the tops of raised surfaces, to better announce their presence to others in the area. That's right, they're poop exhibitionists.

And let's also not discuss how easily one might place several of these droppings into a pretty-looking box to create the worst Valentine's Day practical joke of all time.

> "Square Poo," Museum Victoria, museumvictoria.com

A sixty-year-old woman in Australia whom reports described as an "exotic pet lover" was given a camel in 2007. Maybe the press was having a little fun with that description, because not long afterward she died when the camel attempted to have sex with her. It was extremely unfortunate yet not entirely unexpected, as the camel had been previously known to straddle the family goat.

Some say that the goat had previously voiced concerns about the camel's rapacious behavior, but due to a history of prostitution it was ignored by authorities.

❯"Humped to Death by a Pet Camel," *Metro*, metro.co.uk

Sun bears (*Helarctos malayanus*) are the smallest members of the ursine community, but they have the largest teeth and Freddy Krueger–esque sickles for hands. They are also far and away the most aggressive type of bear, and are known to attack without cause. To aid in their brawling adventures, they have loose, flappy skin (like one of those wrinkly shar-pei dogs). And for no discernible reason whatsoever, among their numerous battle-worthy adaptations is a lolling, 10-inch-long tongue.

Actually, the tongue is used "to get at honey," which sounds extremely dirty, so I'm not going to get into it.

❯"Sun Bear," The Animal Files, theanimalfiles.com

The duckbill platypus is a goofy and adorable mishmash of whimsy. And it also has venomous spurs on its feet that can cause excruciating pain. And since the toxin contained within the spurs is highly resistant to medication, those whom the platypus assaults may be left incapacitated for weeks. There are only a few mammals that are venomous in this way, and just one that looks like a duck got drunk with a gerbil one night, so I guess the platypus at least deserves some sort of award for originality.

Or it could be exhibit number one in the case for compelling Mother Nature to seek professional help for her substance abuse issues.

❯"Unlocking the Mystery of the Duck-Billed Platypus's Venom," American Chemical Society, acs.org

The echidna, a vaguely hedgehog-like mammal, has a face like an anteater, lays eggs like a reptile, has a pouch like a kangaroo, can sense electrical fields like a shark, and is covered in spines like a porcupine. But the one thing that makes it truly unique is that underneath all of that, there's a spectacular, four-headed penis—with the heads rotating in and out of service so they can more efficiently serve the needs of the female's multiple vaginas.

This fact is also the main piece of evidence in Ron Jeremy's current legal struggle to have his nickname legally changed from "The Hedgehog" to "The Echidna."

❯"Four-Headed Echidna Penises under the Microscope for Queensland Captive Breeding Program," Australian Broadcasting Corporation, abc.net.au

The dignified whiskers on mustached tamarins may make them look like a whimsical combination of Victorian gentleman and silly monkey, but these primates aren't nearly as goofy as their appearance might suggest. In fact, they're more like Spartans, at least where child rearing is concerned. If a mother tamarin decides that one of her offspring is a little too runty for her liking, she simply tosses it out of a tree to its death. That is, if she doesn't bite it in the head and eat the baby's brain instead.

❯ "Scientists Rush to Understand the Murderous Mamas of the Monkey World," *Time*, time.com

Between the nonstop poop-slinging, public masturbation, and now this, can we finally get zoos to institute a ratings system, with every monkey house getting a solid XXX?

Giraffes don't reproduce very often (the logistics alone are pretty daunting), and there's only a very narrow window in which the females are even willing to mate. A very delicate dance of seduction must take place before they allow themselves to be romanced by a male, and the way a lady giraffe signals that she's finally ready to take the first steps toward love is by pissing right in his goddamn mouth.

Computer technicians worldwide agree: No creatures on Earth have a more consistently shameful Internet browsing history than giraffes. And possibly Andy Dick.

❯ "Giraffe Reproduction," BioExpedition Publishing, giraffeworlds.com

The solenodon looks like a dopey, foot-long shrew,

and can only be found in remote areas of Cuba and the nearby island of Hispaniola. The way they get their poison into your veins is a bit more spectacular—they use the snake-like method of injecting it via grooves in their teeth.

And here you thought getting accidentally filled with toxins by giant, groovy shrews only happened at Phish concerts.

> "Solenodons: No Bark but Plenty of Venomous Bite," *Smithsonian*, smithsonianmag.com

Capybaras, the most colossal rodents

Mother Nature currently has in production, are interesting for a variety of reasons, and disgusting for one reason in particular (and I'm not talking about the urticating hairs they can fire at will from their butts). To get the most out of the vegetation they're continuously nibbling, capybaras excrete two types of poop. The first is firm, oval-shaped, green, and used for expelling waste. The other is pasty and clear, and serves quite a different purpose—it's for eating again. They're also known for regurgitating their meals to slurp down again as well.

Oh, excuse me. I didn't realize I had walked into a German pornography exhibition. I'll see myself out.

> "Feeding Habits of Capybaras (*Hydrochoerus hydrochaeris*, Linnaeus 1766), in the Ecological Reserve of Taim (ESEC—Taim)—South of Brazil," by L. do Valle Borges and I.G. Colares, *Brazilian Archives and Biology and Technology* (2007), scielo.br

Patricia Wyman was a promising young wildlife biologist who took a job back in 1996 at a wolf exhibit, which was operated by the Haliburton Forest and Wildlife Reserve in Ontario, Canada. This facility was established for educational purposes, and to "foster a better appreciation" of the often vicious, predatory canines. Reports indicate that Ms. Wyman made a concerted effort to establish a rapport with her new charges right from the start, and after only four days on the job, the wolves attacked and killed her.

Investigators were stymied when a brand new Frisbee was later found in the enclosure, mysteriously untouched by the wolves.

❯ "Captive Non-human Socialized Wolves Kill Caretaker in a Canadian Forest and Wildlife Reserve," based on an investigation by Erich Klinghammer, PhD, Director, Institute of Ethology, NAWPF-WOLF PARK

Remember the "Grizzly Man" from a few years back?

The self-proclaimed expert on and friend to grizzly bears? Yeah, he was mauled and eaten. It turns out his story is not unique. Vitaly Nikolayenko of Russia was another self-educated bear expert who believed the furry goliaths were his pals. Right up until they devoured him that very same year.

They say these things always happen in threes, so I guess the remains of an Australian "koala whisperer" must be out there somewhere, still waiting to be found.

❯ "Russian Bear Expert Is Killed in the Wild," *Los Angeles Times*, articles.latimes.com

A woman named Hannah Twynnoy has the posthumous distinction of being the first person to be killed by a tiger in Great Britain. Back in 1703, Twynnoy was working as a bartender in a town called Malmesbury. When a "menagerie" (a sort of old timey traveling zoo) arrived in town, she was warned that she should stop teasing the animals. But she couldn't help herself, and wound up pissing off a tiger so much that it broke out and mauled her to death.

Which some believe was the origin of the famous nursery rhyme "Lady Hannah Got Tore the F*** Up by a Motherf***ing Tiger."

❯"Hannah Twynnoy," Athelstan Museum, athelstanmuseum.org.uk

If you've ever owned a pet in your life that wasn't made out of synthetic fibers and plastic beads, you know that animals can produce a powerful stink. But which species, not counting the ones that reek on purpose just to be assholes, is the global leader in foulness? Well, according to one expert, it's sea lions. San Diego zookeeper Rick Schwartz has worked with a lot of animals over the course of his career, and in his opinion, it's the California sea lion (*Zalophus californianus*) that has the most revolting farts in the animal kingdom.

❯"Which Animal Has the Stinkiest Farts?" Medium, medium.com

Whether it has something to do with their gastrointestinal makeup or is simply because of their proximity to the birthplace of Taco Bell is a matter that is still subject to debate.

Some monkeys are so much like us it's scary. Especially when they form marauding, criminal gangs and terrorize the streets of urban centers. And that's precisely what dozens of young capuchin monkeys have been doing in Rio de Janeiro. Since these poop-flinging ingrates have gotten so used to living off the handouts provided by some monkey-loving humans, whenever the gravy train slows down they'll band together to loot storefronts and even commit home invasions to get the food they believe they're entitled to.

If you're reading any kind of political subtext here I'd appreciate you leaving me out of it. I have neither the time nor the inclination to become a Fox News commentator.

> "Marauding Gangs of Monkeys Invade Rio de Janeiro," Treehugger, treehugger.com

The fluffiest tail in the world belongs to a squirrel in Borneo named *Rheithrosciurus macrotis*. As for the specifics, its tail (when fully poofed) is 130 percent as big as the rest of its body, which makes it the biggest among mammals in terms of snuggly mass. And now for the bad news. Despite the ridiculous proportions of their hindquarters, these squirrels are hardly ever seen in the wild, and all we have to go on in regard to their behavior comes from the locals who claim, that aside from eating nuts and whatnot, that they're also carnivorous. According to one report, "The squirrel waits on a low branch for a deer to pass below, jumps on its back and bites the jugular vein, whereon the deer bleeds to death. Once dead the squirrel proceeds to disembowel the deer and eat the stomach contents, heart, and liver."

On the off chance that this isn't completely bogus, visitors to Borneo should be duly warned about keeping trail mix in the front pockets of their cargo shorts.

❯ "This Squirrel Breaks Record For Tail Size . . . And May Eat Deer's Hearts," Popular Science, popsci.com

In another example of simian shamelessness that happened in Brazil and involved capuchins, a monkey reportedly (and the best part is right on video) broke into a bar, got roaring drunk on stolen rum, and somehow got ahold of a huge kitchen knife. A prolonged standoff with police ensued, and it was only by the grace of God that nobody got monkey-shanked.

By the time this book is published we may already have confirmation, but Rio 2016 is really shaping up to be the most interesting Olympics since the Nazis were running the show.

❯ "Drunk Monkey Armed with Kitchen Knife Chases Bar Patrons," UPI, upi.com

CHAPTER 6

Poisonous Plants and Fearsome Fungi

As long as you avoid stuffing random growths you find in the forest down your throat and carefully sidestep things like poison ivy and cactus you should be pretty safe, right? After all, plants and fungi don't think like you or me. Well, some of them sort of do. It's just not something we can see. There are trees, shrubs, and mushrooms alike with the capacity for murder and devious mayhem. Some can bend insects to their will, and others can devour animals as large as sheep. But again, it's not something you can notice right off the bat. It's subtle. Well, except for the pain some of them can inflict. That can be fairly in-your-face—and sometimes literally *in your face*. So don't ever underestimate the nonanimals around us. Even if they can't intimidate you with a growl or a hiss, they can do some other pretty horrifying things, such as . . .

If you didn't already have the good sense to avoid eating any old fungus you find in the woods, you should be aware that mushrooms have been blamed for the poisoning deaths of many prominent historical figures, from emperors to popes to the Buddha himself. Composer Johann Schobert died of mushroom poisoning along with his family and several of his friends. And perhaps most tragically for fans of wrestling and terrible movies, even Dwayne "The Rock" Johnson's dog, Brutus, succumbed after carelessly snarfing down some toxic pizza toppings that were growing wild in The People's Champion's backyard.

Would it be in bad taste to say that if we "smell what The Rock is cooking" in the near future, it hopefully won't be French bulldog? Sorry, too soon. Too soon.

> ❯ "7 of the World's Most Poisonous Mushrooms," *Encyclopædia Britannica*, britannica.com; "Dwayne 'The Rock' Johnson's Dog Brutus Has Died after Eating a Toxic Mushroom: 'His Soul Is in Pup Heaven,'" *People*, people.com

Should you ever have occasion to vacation in New Zealand, a good rule of thumb might be to photograph the scenery from a distance. But if you insist on indulging your outdoorsy inclinations, be aware that the simple act of walking into a bush can kill you. From the tutu tree (*Coriaria arborea*), with its every surface covered in a convulsion- and suffocation-causing poison, to the stinging hairs of the ongaonga nettle (*Urtica ferox*) that can render one paralyzed (and sometimes dead), the wiser course of action may be to just keep all that L.L.Bean gear in the suitcase and write it off as a loss.

Unless, of course, getting shipped home in a box that has "Died from tutu poisoning" stenciled on the side sounds like an attractive prospect.

> ❯ "Story: Poisonous Plants and Fungi," Te Ara, *The Encyclopedia of New Zealand*, teara.govt.nz

***Physarum polycephalum,* literally meaning "many-headed slime,"** is a slime mold that looks sort of like scrambled eggs and grows on the undersides of logs. To be clear, slime molds have nothing to do with fungus, and in fact we're not precisely sure what the hell they are. What we also have no explanation for is how they are apparently intelligent. This particular slime mold, under the supervision of scientists, has shown the ability to solve problems and work its way through mazes just like any lab rat.

But it's not like we didn't already know that slime had at least some measure of intelligence. I mean, whatever's responsible for making all those comments on YouTube can at least operate a computer.

❯"How Brainless Slime Molds Redefine Intelligence," *Scientific American,* scientificamerican.com

The traditions of Christmas have ancient roots, and the origins of some of them can be surprising. Like "a bunch of dudes high off their gourds on magic mushrooms" surprising. There's a theory that the whole "flying reindeer" thing, for example, came from when Siberian shamans came down people's chimneys to deliver gifts of hallucinatory fungus to their neighbors (it was a strange time). And it may not be mere coincidence that the highly giggle-inducing *Amanita muscaria* mushroom looks exactly like a tree ornament.

❯"Magic Mushrooms May Explain Santa and His 'Flying' Reindeer," Live Science, livescience.com

Not to mention the fact that a "naughty or nice" list is exactly the type of thing a paranoid stoner would dream up.

The durian (*Durio zibethinus*) plant produces a fruit that is known both for being popular among the Whole Foods crowd and also for emitting a smell that's been described as "almost overwhelmingly foul." And the rumors (that eating them can kill you) may in fact be quite true. Not because you run the risk of gagging from the smell of moldy socks, but because durian fruits are packed with sulfur and our bodies have a harder time digesting them than alcohol. Thankfully, however, the urban legend that eating durian while drunk can cause your stomach to explode remains unsubstantiated.

❯ "Death by Durian Fruit?" *Smithsonian,* smithsonianmag.com

Whole Foods shoppers would likely be undeterred even if that rumor were true, just so long as the fruit did its job of making them feel superior for a few moments.

Everyone knows about the Venus flytrap, the creepy little plant that devours flies. What you may not be aware of is that there's a bigger version out there, and it eats rats. The giant pitcher plant can be found in the Philippines, and while it may not have the spectacularly violent qualities of the aforementioned murder-plant, the way it goes about dispatching prey is much more devious. Its shape, as you probably guessed, is that of a pitcher, and inside is a pool of sticky but delicious-smelling liquid. When anything from a tiny bug to a rat enters, the curvature and slippery sides prevent it from ever leaving. Scientifically it's known as *Nepenthes attenboroughii,* and was named for the famed naturalist Sir David Attenborough, who is said to be a great enthusiast of this genus of plants.

So the next time one of those nature shows he hosts comes on the TV, just remember you're watching a dude who gets his jollies from watching rats drown.

❯ "Botanists Discover New Rat-Eating Plant," CNN, cnn.com

The Chernobyl nuclear disaster in 1986 caused a number of unintended repercussions that reverberate to this day. One that you may not be aware of is a black fungus that eats radiation. Found by robotic probes investigating the scene of destruction in 1991, the "radiotrophic" fungus (which looks the same as the kind found on shower curtains) appeared to be the only life form that actually thrived after the catastrophe. Similar species have been found near the site of the doomed Fukushima reactor, and NASA is considering turning it into food for astronauts.

> ❯ "Hungry Fungi Chomp on Radiation," *Nature*, nature.com

Which leads me to believe there may be two things happening we're not being told about: 1.) We've discovered alien life, and it's hostile. 2.) In response we are developing zombie astronauts for deadly spore dispersal.

A "red tide" is something that can occur on just about any coast, and is what happens when a specific type of algae (called dinoflagellates) experience a "bloom" (an exponential increase in their numbers). These events change the color of the water, and spread toxins that can thoroughly eradicate entire populations of whatever marine life happens to be living nearby. When waves kick up those toxins, humans near the shore can breathe them into their respiratory systems. And when enough poison collects inside the local shellfish, a night out at the nearby seafood place can end with sudden death by asphyxiation.

> ❯ "What Causes a Red Tide?" Live Science, livescience.com

And should the condition work in tandem with a severe shellfish allergy, customers are advised to seek shelter under their tables to avoid being pelted by debris from the resulting explosion.

Abrus precatorius is a bean of many names. Crab's eye creeper, love pea, Jamaica wild licorice, and cock's eyes are merely a few. These extremely poisonous, red-and-black "peas" contain a toxin that is just one step below ricin on the toxicity scale, yet they are an ancient symbol of everlasting love in Chinese culture and certainly pretty enough to make jewelry out of. But be careful that you don't prick your finger while stringing together your fetching new necklace, because there is a good possibility you will die. And should you avoid that fate, try not to wear it for too long or you may wind up hospitalized like a British woman was in 2010, due to her nonstop diarrhea, vomiting, and hallucinations.

> "Jequirity Bracelet Danger: British Woman Suffers from Hallucinations and Abscesses Caused by Toxins," *Huffington Post,* huffingtonpost.co.uk

I wonder if this is somehow related to how every time I give my wife a romantic gift, she suddenly comes down with a migraine.

The most toxic of all the Australian "stinging trees" (of which there are an unfortunate multitude) is the gympie gympie (*Dendrocnide moroides*). It doesn't look any more menacing than the average bush, but the leaves are thoroughly laden with hollow, hair-like needles containing a doozy of a neurotoxin. And the simple act of touching the gympie gympie can cause pain so excruciating that people have been known to commit suicide rather than endure it for another minute. Possibly because one of the "cures" is to cover the affected area with hydrochloric acid and then pull out the needles with a hair-removal strip.

> "This Plant's Excruciating Sting Can Drive Humans Mad, or Even Kill," Treehugger, treehugger.com

Well, great. Now I feel like a real jerk about all the whining I did after my wife insisted I get my taint waxed.

Species of the horsetail genus (*Equisetum*) are considered "living fossils." They've been around since the Paleozoic era, when their kind ruled the underbrush. Oddly, horsetails don't reproduce by dropping seeds like most plants. They drop spores like fungi. And unlike anything seen outside of a crappy Netflix horror movie, the spores can walk and jump. It sounds absolutely insane, but these tiny spores have "legs" that react to the level of moisture in the air, causing them to squirm in different directions and flip up into the air to catch wind currents. It's similar to the way human hair can curl when it's humid, only the horsetail spores use the effect to provide locomotion.

Wriggling, dancing spores? It never ceases to amaze how nature always finds a way to give us brand-new phobias.

❯ "Horsetail Plant Spores Use 'Legs' to Walk and Jump," BBC News, bbc.com

Southern Africa is home to the bloodwood tree (*Pterocarpus angolensis*), and there's also a similar version in Australia (*Corymbia opaca*). They're both normal-looking enough, but they were given that creepy name for a good reason. Because should you cut one of them down, or just give one a couple chops, the disturbingly visceral, red sap makes it look like it's bleeding from a gory wound.

Scientists aren't sure, but some believe it may serve as a defense mechanism against nausea-prone woodpeckers and squeamish beavers.

❯ "Cutting a Bloodwood Tree Can Be Disturbing," OutdoorHub, outdoorhub.com

There's also a fungus that responds to the slightest trauma in the same way sexy campers respond to Jason from *Friday the 13th's* machete. The bleeding fairy helmet mushroom (*Mycena haematopus*), or burgundydrop bonnet (we really need to stop letting troubled tweens name mushrooms), looks very much like it's straight out of a fairy tale. And when you pick one out of the ground, and it begins to ooze a dark red substance that looks just like fresh blood, it becomes more like a fairy tale directed by Guillermo del Toro.

But at least pizza restaurant chains can now offer the perfect pizza topping for the newly emerging, thrill–killing cannibal market.

❯ "*Mycena haematopus* (Pers.) P. Kumm.—Burgundydrop Bonnet," First Nature, first-nature.com

The corpse flower (*Amorphophallus titanum*) smells exactly as advertised. Also called the titan arum, it smells like death in order to lure the vilest of pollinators, and it can be found growing in the rainforests of Sumatra. Members of this species are indeed Titans, in that they produce the largest compound flowers of all known plants. Another majestic quality of these plants can be revealed through a translation of their scientific name. *Amorphophallus* is Latin for "huge misshapen penis," and the reason they got that name is because that's exactly what they look like.

❯ "Titan arum (*Amorphophallus titanum*)," Wildscreen Arkive, arkive.org

I'm sure they originally wanted to call it the "giant smelly death cock," but there was probably already a Norwegian metal band out there that beat them to the copyright.

There's a close relation to the corpse flower with an even more spectacularly dreadful designation: *Dracunculus vulgaris*. And if that doesn't give you an inkling as to its overall repugnance, get a load of some of its common names: voodoo lily, dragon arum, snake lily, and stink lily. Like its brethren, it smells like rotting flesh. But its appearance is what really ties everything together. To begin with, the stems are speckled in a way that looks like they're spattered in blood. Then, from the center of the plant arises a black spike that can grow to 4 feet tall, and finally the whole presentation is surrounded by purple petals that give the appearance of a vampire's cowl. Or if you squint your eyes just right, it looks like a dragon. Coincidentally (or not), they despise direct sunlight, and whoa Nelly yes they're poisonous.

Bah, I hear they're not that bad if you raise them next to garlic and occasionally sprinkle them with some Miracle-Gro of the damned.

> "*Dracunculus vulgaris*," Missouri Botanical Garden, missouribotanicalgarden.org

The flower of Hades (*Dactylanthus taylorii*) of New Zealand, on the other hand, doesn't smell like death or even brimstone. The odor it produces is muskier, and resembles the smell that certain small, flying mammals exude after exerting themselves. That's right, they smell like bat sweat. And the reason they do is because it's exactly that variety of filthy, airborne vermin that serves as their pollinators. When the Hades flower blooms on the ground, male bats will become so worked up in a lusty fervor they'll drop out of the sky and start rubbing themselves all over the plant like dry-humping Chihuahuas.

If this seems like an extremely dirty trick on the part of the plant, keep in mind that it's probably a much better option than having sex with another bat.

> "Flower of the Underworld—A Parasitic Treasure," Radio New Zealand, radionz.co.nz

>"Sheep-Eating Plant Opens Up after 15 Years," Seeker, seeker.com

There's an evergreen plant in Chile, *Puya chilensis,* that eats sheep. That wasn't a typo. The top of the plant looks like a medieval mace, and the spines at the base are formidable enough to trap rodents, birds, and yes, sheep. Once their prey has been immobilized, *Puya chilensis* doesn't use the mace-looking part to bash in its skull or anything like that (although that would be pretty awesome), but instead simply waits for it to die of starvation. At which point the plant can absorb the nutrients from the corpse at its leisure.

So the crazy conspiracy theories were right along. WAKE UP, SHEEPLE! I MEAN SHEEP!

The California corn lily (*Veratrum californicum*) is another plant that's bad news for sheep, and

has a much more specific way of screwing with them. If a pregnant ewe eats one of their tasty-looking flowers on exactly the fourteenth day of her lamb's fetal development, that lamb will be born a cyclops. Yes, I know that sounds like space voodoo or something, but it's true. At any other stage, the sheep would suffer no ill effects whatsoever. But it's at exactly this point in time when the baby is susceptible to a particular chemical within the plant that results in the aforementioned hideousness, a condition technically known as holoprosencephaly.

One can only imagine what kind of monster comes out when it's on the thirteenth day, and a Friday.

>"The Curious Case of the One-Eyed Sheep," *Forbes,* forbes.com; "False Hellebore (*Veratrum californicum*)," United States Department of Agriculture, ars.usda.gov

Fig trees are pollinated by a certain type of wasp, and in return the wasps get to lay their eggs in the trees' fruit. But if a fig tree senses that the wasps aren't doing a good enough job on their end, they'll retaliate by purposely dropping their figs early, thereby killing the baby wasps within.

> "Study: Trees Retaliate When Fig Wasps Don't Service Them," *Cornell Chronicle*, cornell.edu

Hey, a deal's a deal. And it's not like trees have hearts, literally or figuratively, so the wasps should have known what they were getting into when they signed the contract.

They say eating apples on a daily basis serves as a natural repellant to members of the medical community or some crap like that, but eating too many of them can kill you. Well, eating too much of anything can kill you, obviously. But not everything contains amygdalin, a sugar and *cyanide* based concoction, like apple seeds definitely do.

> "Cyanide in Fruit Seeds: How Dangerous Is an Apple?" *Guardian*, theguardian.com

Sure, you have to eat a ton of them for death to occur, but it definitely raises some questions as to what exactly that lowlife Johnny Appleseed was up to.

The largest living thing that ever existed is a fungus, and it lives in Oregon. The organism covers 4 square miles of earth, and some estimates place it as being 8,650 years old. The species in question is called *Armillaria solidipes* (formerly *ostoyae*), and the only evidence that this leviathan dwells beneath comes during the autumn months, when it sends probes known as "honey mushrooms" up to the surface to further spread its influence. For the rest of the year it remains completely hidden underground. Waiting.

> "Strange but True: The Largest Organism on Earth Is a Fungus," *Scientific American*, scientificamerican.com

Locals often refer to the organism as the "Humongous Fungus," which is just hilarious. Because it rhymes, I guess. Remember, this is Oregon we're talking about here, so they're probably really, really high.

One plant whose scientific name alone should let you know it's up to no good would be *Salvinia molesta*. And molest it does, possessing a reputation as "the world's worst weed" and a record of successful invasiveness to boot. It's gradually choking the life out of lakes in places like Australia by blocking out sunlight with its sheer numbers, and piling up to the point where rivers can no longer move. These lovely weeds are also doing the exact opposite of helping the world by creating the perfect breeding grounds for mosquitos.

And with a name like that, you should probably never wade into waters where these weeds are present without at least several thick pairs of underwear.

❯"Weed Management Guide: Salvinia (*Salvinia molesta*)," Australian Government, environment.gov.au; "Aquatic Invasive Species: Giant Salvinia," State of Indiana, in.gov

Anyone with even an ounce of common sense knows enough to avoid poison ivy. And it may not come as a shock that anyone foolish enough to actually eat the leaves of that plant might experience some rather unpleasant outcomes (like a throat swollen shut). But one thing you might not immediately realize is how dangerous poison ivy can be if it accidentally finds its way into a bonfire. Should that occur, inhaling the smoke produced by burning this noxious weed can affect your lungs and make it very difficult to breathe. Like, ever again.

❯"Poison Ivy," ScienceDaily, sciencedaily.com

Which is why you should definitely avoid any bargain vape shop where the owner is known to cut corners and seems to scratch himself a lot.

Telegraph plants (*Codariocalyx motorius*) are also known as "dancing grass." Not because they sway seductively in the breeze, but because their leaves move around even if there's no wind whatsoever. One of the few plants in existence capable of rapid movement (the Venus flytrap being another), the telegraph plant also responds rapidly to light and sound in a way that seems impossible for a shrub. Some believe the reason they jig around is so that they can more efficiently take advantage of available sunlight. But another theory suggests they may simply have evolved this ability to creep the hell out of any animal that might want to eat them.

> "Bloom of the Week—The Telegraph Plant," University of Virginia, people.virginia.edu

Now if they can just evolve a long, high-pitched cackle, their habitats would be immune to human encroachment for all of eternity.

It's weird to think of a lowly mushroom (especially one that we eat on a regular basis) as being carnivorous, but researchers describe *Pleurotus ostreatus*, or the oyster mushroom, as a "silent assassin." First, these mushrooms produce a chemical that attracts tiny worms called nematodes. These creatures are subsequently exposed to a toxin containing a protein called pleurotolusin, and once this protein comes in contact with living cells, it proceeds to carve holes in them like a "cookie cutter." Obviously this is fairly disastrous for the worms, and once they're dead the mushroom simply absorbs the nutrients from their corpses.

There aren't many occasions in life to sympathize with a worm. But it's understandable if, the next time you order stir-fry, you chomp down on those mushrooms with just a little bit of hate in your heart.

> "Carnivorous Mushroom Kills with 'Cookie Cutters,'" Nature World News, natureworldnews.com

***Coprinus comatus*, commonly known as shaggy ink cap, lawyer's wig, or shaggy mane,** is another worm-murdering mushroom. They go about their homicidal business a little differently, however, and the way they harvest their victims is by stabbing them with "spiny balls" that grow out of the mushrooms themselves. These burr-like structures pierce and paralyze the nematodes, forcing their innards to squirt out of the wounds. And then the worms are simply digested exactly where they died, and the remnants of their bodies colonized to grow new mushrooms.

Seriously, who knew how much it sucks to be a worm? From these goddamn mushrooms, to sidewalks turning into writhing killing fields after it rains, to being constantly skewered on fishhooks . . . it's like the world is just one huge worm death orgy.

❯ "*Coprinus comatus*: A Basidiomycete Fungus Forms Novel Spiny Structures and Infects Nematode," by H. Luo, M. Mo, X. Huang, X. Li, and K. Zhang, *Mycologia* (2004), ncbi.nlm.nih.gov

When certain types of corn, cotton, and tobacco plants sense that caterpillars are nibbling on their leaves, they will release a chemical that summons parasitic wasps. The wasps are grateful for the opportunity to lay their eggs inside the caterpillars, and the plants can enjoy the fact that their tormentors are about to be devoured from the inside out by voracious larvae.

Tobacco and wasps generally get such a bad rap that it's nice to hear a heart-warming story of friendship like this every once in a while.

❯ "Plants Send SOS When Caterpillars Bite," United States Department of Agriculture, agresearchmag.ars. usda.gov

The copious thorns on bullhorn acacia (*Vachellia cornigera*) are pretty good for keeping unwanted pests from chomping away on its leaves, but not quite good enough. This acacia has evolved to make its thorns hollow, so that they're the perfect nesting place for a particularly sting-happy species of ant. The ant gets to sip on the tasty nectar the tree produces, along with a comfortable place to raise its horrible babies; meanwhile, the acacia has a built-in army of bodyguards, just waiting for the chance to gnaw the head off a cricket or lay into the nose of a cocky goat. As a bonus, it's recently been found that the ants have a particular strain of bacteria on their legs that acts as an antibiotic, thus preventing the acacias from coming down with a nasty, debilitating type of fungus.

As pleasant as all this sounds for both the tree and the ant, you have to imagine the poor squirrels that have to live in that tree are pretty damn depressed.

> "Protect and Survive," *Economist*, economist.com

Cerbera odollam is commonly placed between homes as a fence of sorts in certain parts of India, and is known as the "suicide tree" due the high toxicity of its leaves. And there's no exaggeration where it comes to that name, as it's frequently used as a murder weapon as well as a means of self-destruction. In fact, in one Indian state half of all poisoning cases involve extracts from this tree.

They do say fences make the best neighbors. Or, in this case, organ-melting murder shrubbery.

> "Cerberin: The Heartbreaker of the Suicide Tree," Nature's Poisons, naturespoisons.com

For some inexplicable reason the South American flowering plant *Psychotria elata* has evolved so that its petals arrange themselves to look exactly like an oversized, heavily lipsticked, lustily puckering human mouth. Perhaps there's a variety of butterfly and/or hummingbird down there that enjoys the company of the kind of ladies you might meet at a pool party hosted by Charlie Sheen? That at least could explain why many refer to the plant as "hooker's lips."

❯ "Hooker's Lips Plant—*Psychotria elata*," Seeds of Eaden, seedsofeaden.com

Word has it that Mr. Sheen may actually decorate his home with this particular plant but has to have them delivered at least once per week, usually with an accompanying order of hypoallergenic lubricant.

Skunk cabbage smells about as pleasant as its name implies, and can be found growing wild in bogs and swamps. It is possible to eat them, if that's your thing, but you have to thoroughly cook out the tiny crystals that are contained in the leaves. Because if you don't, they'll perforate your mouth like a handful of glass. Now here's the best part: Skunk cabbages often grow intermixed with another plant called the white hellebore. Their shoots look very similar to one another, but should you eat some hellebore by mistake it won't matter how much you cooked it—it'll still probably put you in the morgue.

❯ "Skunk Cabbage (*Symplocarpus foetidus*)," Virginia Native Plant Society, vnps.org

Just to be safe, you should avoid bringing kimchee to work and leaving it in the heating ducts for weeks. I'm not sure if that applies directly to skunk cabbage or not, but that's what my boss told me. And that if I did that again I'd definitely be fired.

The hallucinogenic qualities of catnip (*Nepeta cataria*) affect some felines more than others, and most of the time it's a harmless way for pets to let off steam. But some cats can be allergic to it, and eating it can cause your cat to start violently puking and spraying diarrhea. But you might want to wait until she comes down and falls asleep before taking away her fix, because a few felines love catnip so much that they'll become violently aggressive toward anything and anyone attempting to take the source of their high away.

> ❯ "Why Catnip Isn't for Every Cat," Petango, petango.com

That reminds me a lot of a problem I used to have whenever I was at parties in college. The spraying diarrhea thing, I mean.

Zonal geraniums (*Pelargonium x hortorum*) really hate it when pesky Japanese beetles (*Popillia japonica*) chomp away on their leaves. So they figured out a way to pay them back in spades. To deter said chomping, these plants have evolved the ability to produce a certain type of chemical that causes the beetles to lose the use of their hind legs, essentially rendering them paraplegics.

Whoa, don't you think you're going a little overboard there, chief? Does Home Depot sell any anger management fertilizer in their gardening section?

❯ "Rare Excitatory Amino Acid from Flowers of Zonal Geranium Responsible for Paralyzing the Japanese Beetle," by C.M. Ranger, R.E. Winter, A.P. Singh, M.E. Reding, J.M. Frantz, J.C. Locke, and C.R. Krause, *Proceedings of the National Academy of Sciences of the United States* (2011), ncbi.nlm.nih.gov

In 2014 a British gardener died of multiple organ failure after merely brushing up against a flower of the aconitum plant on his millionaire employer's estate. Sometimes called monkshood or devil's helmet, aconitum is common in the northern hemisphere and has a rather sordid history of being used by hunters to kill wolves, leopards, and mice (which is probably why some other nicknames for the plant are wolfsbane, leopardsbane, and mousebane). Even more disturbingly, the poison from aconitum has been effective in killing bears and even whales. And let's not get into why yet another name for the plant is "women's bane."

One suggested name, "the Sean Connery slapweed," while highly descriptive of the inherent misogyny of the plant, was presumably scrapped due to legal considerations.

❯ "Gardener Dies 'after Brushing Against Deadly Wolfsbane Flower' on Millionaire's Estate," *Independent,* independent.co.uk; "A Pacific Eskimo Invention in Whale Hunting in Historic Times," by R.F. Heizer, *American Anthropologist* (1943), escholarship. org; "Aconitum," Encyclopedia of Life, eol.org

The delightful-looking and delicious-sounding buttercup flower can be found growing all over the globe. It's also great for fatally poisoning livestock. So go ahead and hold one under a child's chin for some innocent fun, but for God's sake don't put it in your mouth unless you're looking for a sudden case of diarrhea, bloody urine, convulsions, and death.

So why do we use "buttercup" as a term of endearment again? You may as well tell your kids to "eat shit and die" before you head off to work in the mornings.

❯ "*Ranunculus acris*, Meadow Buttercup," The Poison Garden, thepoisongarden.co.uk

You've surely seen plenty of lichens, the crusty, vaguely infectious-looking growths on trees and rocks, even if you're not among the snooty few who can pronounce the word correctly (it's "likens"). And you probably assumed they were organisms completely unto themselves, like a mushroom is a mushroom, a goat is a goat, and so on. But in fact they're more of an interspecies cooperative, or a mighty morphin' team of lower life forms. A lichen results when bacteria or algae engage in a symbiotic relationship with fungus, forming composite organisms that generally look like a colossally bad idea for a pizza topping. But don't worry; they're perfectly harmless. Except for that one variety that's so noxious that people in Europe used to stuff it inside the carcasses of reindeer to poison wolves. Or the one that some Native American tribes used to make poison arrows. Or the one that killed 300 elk in Wyoming in the space of a year.

> "Lichens—Did You Know?" United States Department of Agriculture Forest Service, fs.fed.us; "*Letharia vulpina*: Wolf Lichen," Encyclopedia of Life, eol.org

Still, I'd be shocked if Whole Foods didn't try to convince hipsters that "lichens are nature's gummy bears" at some point.

The Brazilian sandbox tree (*Hura crepitans*) has an . . . interesting method of seed dispersal: The fruit it produces explodes. Not that you'd want to try to pick one up in the first place, since the fruit of these "dynamite trees" also has a toxic sap that causes welts to form immediately upon contact with human skin. Anyway, the fruit detonations (which are so loud that they've been mistaken for gunfire) can send its seeds flying outward in a 40-foot radius, which is bad news for everyone except some hungry birds and primates. Thus, they have another, less combative nickname: "monkey's dinner bell."

> "*Hura crepitans*: Sandbox Tree," Encyclopedia of Life, eol.org

You have to admit, watching monkeys try to deal with exploding fruit would be some sweet revenge for when they whipped feces at your face that one time at the zoo.

Taking your dog for a walk around the lake can sometimes be a dangerous proposition for all parties involved, and I'm not talking about encounters with surly geese. In fact, any body of water in the world might potentially be a breeding ground for toxic algae, which can be fatal to both dogs and humans. You can't really tell for sure if a lake or pond is the dog-murdering kind from color or smell alone, so it's probably best to avoid the water entirely if you see scum forming on the surface.

And that can apply for human scum as well, like the middle-aged men who insist on wearing Speedos in public and hitting on young girls.

> "Toxic Algae in Lakes and Ponds Can Kill Your Dog," Petful, petful.com

When the sap from a giant hogweed plant (*Heracleum mantegazzianum*) oozes onto human flesh, a reaction occurs that might make you sympathize with a vampire's natural fear of UV rays. Because as soon as sunlight enters the mix, painful blisters start to erupt where the sap made contact with the skin. These are no ordinary blisters—they can lead to necrosis, and the scars that are left behind can last up to six years. The condition can also result in the sufferer developing a long-term sensitivity to light, and God help the poor idiot who rubs the stuff in his eyes. Furthermore, while this plant used to be located solely in the Caucasus Mountains, between the Black and Caspian seas, it's since invaded the United States and is currently terrorizing states from Oregon to New York.

> "Giant Hogweed: 8 Facts You Must Know about the Toxic Plant," CBS News, cbsnews.com

In olden times these symptoms must have seemed so mysterious that many women were probably burned at the stake in the mistaken belief that Dracula had given them magic herpes.

> "Australia's Wildfires: Are Eucalyptus Trees to Blame?" Live Science, livescience.com

The oil in eucalyptus trees is so flammable that wildfires can cause them to explode. This seemingly self-destructive adaptation has led Australians to refer to them as "gasoline trees." However, since eucalyptus trees are so adept at recovering after a blaze, with seedlings that thrive in "freshly-burned, ash-rich soils," it's believed that they might be blowing up on purpose. Which would mean that they're knowingly spraying burning sap onto other nearby tree species, so that their competition will be engulfed and consumed in a fiery act of maliciousness.

And when the cuddly koalas that live in those eucalyptus trees start detonating, one after the other, it may just be part of a larger psychological campaign.

The beautiful and delicate *Nerium oleander* flower would be the envy of any horticulturist's prized collection—if it didn't put the lives of everyone in its immediate vicinity at mortal risk, that is. This shrub from the dogbane family is one of the most toxic plants in existence, and every single bit of it, from the flowers to the stem to the sap, can be deadly. Even inhaling the smoke from a burning *Nerium oleander* can seriously mess you up, and there have been a few reported cases of ignorant campers winding up in the hospital after cooking hot dogs on its sticks. Even the honey that's produced by the bees that pollinate this plant is poisonous.

My God. I had no idea those honey-glazed weenie hors d'oeuvres with the little oleander toothpicks I served those Boy Scouts were poisonous, officer.

> "Acute Cardiac Toxicity of *Nerium oleander/indicum* Poisoning (Kaner) Poisoning," by I. Khan, C. Kant, A. Sanwaria, and L. Meena, *Heart Views* (2010), ncbi.nlm.nih.gov

Making the Venus flytrap look like a chump,
bladderworts (genus *Utricularia*) have the most sophisti-
cated carnivorous trapping system among plants. Their
genus includes species that live underwater, and what
they do is form empty, transparent, bean-like pouches
(or bladders) that essentially operate like trapdoors,
with tiny hairs near the opening to serve as a triggering
mechanism. When an insect, tadpole, or even a fish rubs
up against the hairs, the plant creates a vacuum effect
that sucks the creature inside the bean, which immediately seals up to eliminate any hope of escape. The entire
process, from the triggering to the sucking to the sealing,
takes about half a millisecond.

*A bean that sucks? That's pretty different than the ones I'm used to. So if you
put these things in a burrito, would all the alternating farting and sucking create a tiny black hole or something?*

> "Carnivorous Bladderworts Catch Meals with Vacuum Power," *Wired*, wired.com

**A chytrid fungus called *Batrachochytrium dendro-
batidis*** is currently threatening one-third of the entire
world's amphibian species with annihilation. What it does
is cause a disease that affects the skin, which happens to
be the organ that amphibians use to drink and breathe.
There's one type of toad that seems to have built up some
immunity to the disease, but not every amphibian has had
the time to evolve defenses. As the chytrid fungus spreads
across the globe, the frog apocalypse may soon be upon us.

> "Scientists Make
Breakthrough in
Fight Against
Deadly Amphibian
Fungus," *Guardian*,
theguardian.com

*Thank goodness scientists are hard at work developing a vaccine, and not
wasting their time curing cancer or anything stupid like that.*

Eucalyptus deglupta trees can be found in a select few tropical regions east of Indonesia and can reach a height of more than 200 feet. And what's also notable about them is their unusual bark, which is multicolored in various shades of red, blue, green, brown, purple, and orange. This bizarre coloration on their trunks is why they're commonly referred to as "rainbow eucalyptus." They might seem like they'd make for a delightful addition to your backyard, up until you come to find that they double their size every year until you have a tree that looks like the world's biggest gay pride totem pole.

❯"Nature Blows My Mind! Rainbow Colored Trees Grow over 200 Feet Tall," Treehugger, treehugger.com

Loggers presumably give them a wide berth, out of fear of being accused of perpetrating a hate crime.

The "green menace" that is the invasive kudzu plant has strangled competing vegetation in states like Alabama and Georgia. Thanks to a nearly unstoppable capacity for rapid expansion and reproduction, kudzu vines have been suffocating native trees to near-extinction, while simultaneously overtaking and enveloping anything in their path that doesn't have the good sense to get out of the way. Reportedly, an entire bridge in Tennessee was smothered to the point where you wouldn't even know there was a bridge there in the first place. Herbicides and clippers can't keep up with the ever-advancing menace, and it's more than earned the nickname of "the vine that ate the South."

❯"'The Green Menace' Grows Near Voracious Kudzu Vine Is Taking a Bite of Phila," Philly.com, philly.com

Eventually it will reach New Jersey, where the toxic waste will either kill it or mutate it into an abomination that begins devouring the populace. So, win–win.

The *Hydnora africana* plant is awful on a variety of levels. First off, it's as close as nature has ever come to replicating Audrey II from *Little Shop of Horrors*. Moreover, it doesn't bother with the whole photosynthesis thing, since it does just fine making a living as a crippling parasite of other plants. It also smells like crap (on purpose), in order to entice dung beetles to enter its hideous flowers. It doesn't eat the beetles, like one might assume, but instead "imprisons" them for pollination purposes. (The flowers are easy to enter but very difficult to leave, just like a certain motel frequented by roaches.) After a few hours the beetles are eventually released, but not until *Hydnora africana* has made sure they've got the maximum amount of stinky pollen plastered on their backs.

> "*Hydnora africana*," Botanical Society of America, botany.org

Yeah, it's not like dung beetles don't suffer enough humiliation in life or anything. Now they have to live with the fact a plant just made them its bitch.

Many consider the manchineel (*Hippomane mancinella*) to be the world's most dangerous tree.
It ranges from Florida to South America, and the Spanish conquistadors called it the "little apple of death." Reason being, the tasty-looking fruit they produce can be fatally poisonous to eat. But aside from that, you can also die merely by brushing against the sap, leaves, and/or bark.

The Snow White story would have been a whole lot different if it took place in South America, apparently. There would definitely have been a lot more dead dwarves.

> "Why Manchineel Might Be Earth's Most Dangerous Tree," Mother Nature Network, mnn.com

The Javan cucumber (*Alsomitra macrocarpa*) produces "flying" seeds that look like huge, translucent space bats. They have a wingspan of over 5 inches, and can easily be mistaken for some kind of radioactively mutated butterfly as they dip and climb through the air. Why is nature tormenting us in this way, you may ask? Well, it's all about dispersal. Those aforementioned terror seeds are so aerodynamic that they can glide, whether or not there's any wind, for miles before they eventually touch down.

> The Triumph of Seeds: How Grains, Nuts, Kernels, Pulses, and Pips Conquered the Plant Kingdom and Shaped Human History by Thor Hanson

I have no idea what the cucumbers these turn into look like, but I can definitely see marketing "flying pickles" as a means of nonviolent conflict resolution.

Hikers in the United States might be tempted to nibble on wild onions they find growing out in the wilderness. But unless you're some expert in onion-ology or whatever, it's probably a bad idea. Because they often grow next to and look just like a plant called a death camas. And with a name like that you can probably guess what's coming next. That's right, SLUDGE. Or rather, "Salivation, Lacrimation, Urination, Defecation, GI upset, and Emesis."

> "Don't Eat the Death Camas . . . or 'Death' Anything," Nature's Poisons, naturespoisons.com

Oh yeah, and also "Death." So basically, you're SLUDGED.

In 2002 the authorities in Northern Queensland, Australia, legislated the removal of every single tree of a certain type from their beaches in order to avoid lawsuits. Why? Because the families of dead tourists were constantly seeking compensation after their relatives got their heads bashed in by falling coconuts. These weren't frivolous complaints by any means. Approximately 150 people around the world die in this manner every year.

> "Trees Must Go as Queensland Guards Against Death by Coconut," Telegraph, telegraph.co.uk

I once tried to include "death by coconut" in my family's insurance plan, but it really had more to do with my wife's baking skills.

The borrachero (loosely translated as "get you drunk") tree is native to South America, and its seeds are used to make a drug called scopolamine. Also known as "the devil's breath," it's great for easing nausea symptoms, and has even been used by NASA (to help keep their astronauts' helmets from filling up with barf, I guess). Scopolamine is also a mind-altering substance, and is used by criminals to turn their victims into willing "zombies" who will follow any command, no matter how horrible.

Studies have shown that similar circumstances can occur when children force their parents to listen to the Frozen soundtrack again and again and again.

❯ "Three Arrested in Paris over 'Devil's Breath' Drug That Turns Victims Into Willing 'Zombies,'" *Telegraph*, telegraph.co.uk

---

The resin spurge is a Moroccan shrub that superficially resembles a cactus. The spikes aren't the issue with the spurge, however. It's the fact it exudes a chemical called resiniferatoxin that is rather . . . spicy. For perspective, it's 3,000 times hotter than the chemical used in pepper spray. On the Scoville scale—the system of heat measurement on which peppers are judged—jalapeños come in at around 2,500–5,000 Scoville heat units, and habaneros at 100,000–577,000. Pretty impressive, right? Resiniferatoxin tips the scale right off the cliff at a tongue-obliterating 16,000,000,000 Scoville heat units.

❯ "Hottest Chemical?—Resiniferatoxin Is a Thousand Times Hotter Than Capsaicin," About Education, chemistry. about.com; "Fact File—The Scoville Heat Scale," Chilliworld, chilliworld.com

So if you happen to get some hot sauce from Taco Bell that says "Spurge" on the packet, you might want to put on some rubber pants and make sure a paramedic is en route.

A handy item for torturing your enemies is *dief-fenbachia*, a flowering plant that grows in an area ranging from Mexico to Argentina. This waxy shrub is just as popular today as a houseplant as it was hundreds of years ago among slave owners in the West Indies for punishing servants. If one of those aforementioned unfortunates happened to become "unruly," *dieffenbachia* would be stuck in their mouths, and the pain and swelling would render them unable to speak. Due to this phenomenon, the common name of the shrub became "dumb cane." And another historical application of its peculiar properties was to silence witnesses to crimes.

And presumably as an ingredient to every meal served when spouses invited unwanted family members to stay over for the weekend.

> *Poisoning Plants, Mycotoxins, and Related Toxins*, edited by Franklin Riet-Correa, Jim Pfister, Ana Lucia Schlid, and Terrie Wierenga

A fungus with the catchy name of Tropical Race 4 may soon render the bananas we get from the grocery store extinct. And it wouldn't be the first time something like this has happened. Years ago another fungus completely exterminated the Gros Michel banana, which was the most widely consumed at the time. Now growers are already experimenting with other varieties of the fruit to replace the dying one, which means that soon the taste our children associate with bananas will be completely different than ours.

It's a sad state of affairs to be sure, but it does raise hopes that a fungus that targets Brussels sprouts for extermination may one day appear.

> "Our Favorite Banana May Be Doomed; Can New Varieties Replace It?" National Public Radio, npr.org

CHAPTER 7

Ravenous Reptiles and Appalling Amphibians

Both reptiles and amphibians are popular pets you'd probably be wise to avoid. Granted, not all of them are glistening with poison or sharp of fang. But as any reasonable person would likely agree, you should never place your trust in any creature with an inherent aversion to snuggling. We use the term *reptilian* to describe those among us who display a cold, calculating capacity for evil acts, and no one in recorded history has ever been flattered to be called a toad. To compare someone to these organisms is invariably an insult, and that's not by accident. All you need is a few moments spent bearing witness to the dispassionate way a snake dispatches its prey, the spectacle of a lizard mutilating itself for defense, or the doll-eyed casualness of a frog doing something incredibly distasteful with its tongue to know that you're in the presence of an animal that cannot love. And neither do they wish to be loved, for their motives are base and terrible. And there can be little counterpoint to this reality when you consider such activities as . . .

The "horror frog" (***Trichobatrachus robustus***) is aptly named, seeing as how the way it defends itself seems more like a scene from one of the Hellraiser movies than anything based in reality. Like most amphibians, they aren't born with claws. So, when the need arises, they will purposefully break their own bones, which then emerge out of their skin, to create them. Oh, did I mention they're sometimes called "hairy frogs"? That's because they're also hairy.

>"'Horror Frog' Breaks Own Bones to Produce Claws," *New Scientist*, newscientist.com

Instead of croaking, I assume they spend all night whispering, "THERE IS NO GOD."

The Iberian ribbed newt (***Pleurodeles waltl***) responds to threats in a ghoulish fashion. This amphibian's defensive technique is to expand its ribcage until the bones burst right through the skin. Following this action, a poison seeps out of the holes created by the jutting ribs and coats the jagged points. Needless to say, this makes the Iberian newt a rather unpalatable meal for most predators.

Or at least the ones that don't really care for their lunch treating the inside of their throats like Freddy Krueger treated Johnny Depp.

>"Spanish Ribbed Newt," Dudley Zoological Gardens, dudleyzoo.org.uk

The inland taipan (*Oxyuranus microlepidotus*) doesn't seem like a very spectacular name for the most venomous snake in the world, but nonetheless, that is the reptile that holds that distinction. To absolutely no one's surprise, this species hails from Australia, and a single drop of venom from their fangs is enough to kill 100 men (or 250,000 mice). Their cousin, the coastal taipan, lives nearby but isn't nearly as deadly (although it's reportedly more vicious). Shamefully, it's only the third most venomous land snake in the world.

A fact that the inland versions presumably never fail to mention at twenty-year class reunions. Even though they generally peak too early, never go to college like the coastal ones, and usually wind up managing a shoe store in the mall.

❯"Inland Taipan," BBC, bbc.co.uk; "Mystery Over Boy Bitten by World's Most Venomous Snake," *Sunday Morning Herald*, smh.com.au; "Coastal Taipan," Queensland Museum, qm.qld.gov.au

The goliath frog (*Conraua goliath*) from West Africa is the world's largest frog by a long shot. They're bigger than most Chihuahuas. In addition to the standard froggy fare of bugs and such, goliath frogs are sizable enough to eat crabs, turtles, snakes, and bats. A frog of this magnitude must certainly have an impressively resounding croak, right? Well, they actually can't croak at all due to the lack of a vocal sac. What they do instead is hold their mouths open and emit unnerving, whistling howls.

❯"*Conraua goliath*," Animal Diversity Web, animaldiversity.org

Honestly, I can't think of a more perfect co-star should Rosie O'Donnell ever be cast as a princess in a Disney movie.

The Gila monster (*Heloderma suspectum*) is the only venomous lizard in North America, which is something you're probably aware of if you've ever been to any store in the southwestern United States that sells postcards. They don't have hollow fangs like a snake, however, so the way they get the poison into your bloodstream is by snapping on with their incredibly strong jaws, and then grinding the toxins into your flesh. According to a 1910 newspaper clipping, at least one Native American tribe found this to be such a dreadful scenario that they had a legend that stated: "the most fearful vengeance that may come to the spirit bodies of bad Indians after this life, is to be bitten by a red Gila monster that roams, unseen by mortal eyes, over the adobe plains."

To honor this legend, it's possible modern tribes may be using some form of this retribution against casino tourists caught counting cards at the blackjack table.

❯ "Gila Monsters and Beaded Lizards," *Reptiles Magazine*, reptilesmagazine.com

If somebody told you there was a snake that had tentacles, and that those tentacles grew out of its face, you'd probably immediately change seats on the subway to put space between yourself and the schizophrenic hobo. But in fact there is something called the tentacled snake (*Erpeton tentaculatum*), and its name is not a sick joke. Its tentacles don't have suckers on them but are used to sense fish in the Southeast Asian waters where they lurk.

"Come on, it's not that weird, really," said the acolyte of the Great Old One Cthulhu as he did his part to lull a doomed humanity into a false sense of complacency.

❯ "Tentacled Snakes," Vanderbilt University, as.vanderbilt.edu

Speaking of hideous snake mutations, there's also a serpent from Iran that was only just described in 2006. The spider-tailed horned viper (*Pseudocerastes urarachnoides*) has a name that sounds like a child trying to describe a recurring nightmare, but this species actually does have horns. Oh, were you curious about that other part too? Well, you know how some snakes have rattles? This one has something sort of like that, only it's in the shape of a tarantula.

Psychiatrists who specialize in phobias refer to this sort of creature as "Screw it, I give up."

❯ "Incredible Snake Uses Tail That Looks Like a Spider to Lure in Prey," *Daily Mirror*, mirror.co.uk

Some frogs can arguably be considered "cute," but it can be hard to maintain that opinion after watching them eat. And if their fleshy (sometimes projectile) tongues and the panicked struggling of live prey descending into their gullets isn't enough to put you off your feed, here's another aspect to consider. In order to assist in the swallowing of stubborn, wriggling prey, frogs use their eyeballs to help push food down their throats. Using X-ray technology, scientists found that the eyes actually migrate down toward the frog's esophagus to accomplish this task.

❯ "Frogs Use Their Eyes to Push Food Down While Swallowing," *Discover*, discovermagazine.com

For bonus fun, just think of it as the amphibian equivalent of stomping on an incriminating Steve Buscemi to force him into the wood chipper.

Satanic leaf-tailed geckos (*Uroplatus phantasticus*) may be harmless to humans, but they look like wee servants of Beelzebub himself. The bizarre camouflage that's intended to help them blend in with trees conversely makes them look like they're from another planet entirely. They look so much like mythological beasts pulled straight out of a fantasy novel that when someone Photoshopped a pair of wings on one and posted it on the Internet, *Game of Thrones* fans briefly lost their goddamn minds, thinking that dragons were real.

❯ "Satanic Leaf-Tailed Gecko (*Uroplatus phantasticus*)," Wildscreen Arkive, arkive.org; "*Game of Thrones* Fans Freak Out over Fake Photo of 'Real Dragon,'" CBC, cbc.ca

It was reminiscent of the time Star Wars *fans followed Bob Costas around, mistakenly believing him to be a partially shaved Ewok.*

Chelus fimbriata, **or the matamata turtle (Spanish for "It kills! It kills!")** is pretty much hands down the most bizarre turtle in existence. Its head, which looks like a massive, diseased turd, can stretch out hideously like a snake's. A haphazard array of "protuberances, warts, skin fringes, and ridges" all over its body and shell simply adds to the overall repugnance. It hardly ever does much in the way of swimming, or moving at all for that matter, since all it has to do to capture its meals is lie underwater, hold its head up, and suck. They probably won't actually murder you, though.

❯ "Matamata Turtle (*Chelus fimbriatus*)," Atlantic City Aquarium, acaquarium.com

Unless you should happen upon two of them mating, at which point you may lose all faith in a loving God, and subsequently the will to live.

We all know that frogs are great at croaking, but were you aware that some of them can scream? One of the most frightening examples is the smoky jungle frog (*Leptodactylus pentadactylus*) from Costa Rica. If being friggin' huge (over 7 inches), with toxic skin and the ability to blow up like a party balloon isn't enough to ward off a predator, they'll emit a high-pitched shriek that sounds just like a demonic newborn baby. And if that still isn't enough, smoky jungle frogs have one final trick up their sleeves. Remember that toxin skin from before? Somehow they can vaporize the toxin, meaning they can poison your ass without even touching you.

> ❯ "Smoky jungle frog," BBC, bbc.co.uk; "Costa Rica's Smoky Jungle Frog," Go Visit Costa Rica, govisitcostarica.com

Which is essentially the same principle by which certain young men are somehow able to repel women solely through the overuse of scented body sprays.

There's a lizard that's also proficient in blood-curdling screams. Leopard geckos (*Eublepharis macularius*) are crepuscular, which sounds like an insult someone wearing a top hat and a monocle might call you, but it actually means they're most active at twilight. In the deserts of Pakistan and Northern India, this is when the shrieking begins. Inexplicably, these lizards are quite popular in the pet trade.

> ❯ "Leopard Gecko Caresheet," The Gecko Spot, thegeckospot.net

Presumably among apartment-dwelling practical jokers who get a kick out of making their neighbors think there's a serial killer in the building.

The *Dasypeltis* genus includes several species of egg-eating snakes. And while they're completely harmless, they make up for it by being extraordinarily gross. Just as advertised, the only things they eat are eggs, and they eat them whole—even if the eggs are much bigger than their heads. It's quite a sight to behold, and if you've ever seen footage of a snake unhinging its jaws in order to eat a large rat, just multiply the cringe factor by about twelve. They don't have fangs where you would normally expect but instead have teeth at the back of their throats. You know, to break the eggs once they're finally done disturbing everyone around them by doing that carnival freak show routine in the first place. And they refuse to eat any other way—if you offer one some egg in a bowl, it will adamantly refuse.

You have to admire them, honestly. It's rare to see that level of commitment to being repugnant since Jersey Shore went off the air.

> "Dasypeltis," Dasypeltis.com, dasypeltis.com

The Asian water monitor (*Varanus salvator*) is second only to the Komodo dragon in terms of absurdly gigantic lizards. The largest one found was upward of 11 feet long, and the common term in Thailand for them is "hia," which can be roughly translated as "damn bastard." The reason the locals there might not feel too fondly toward water monitors may have something to do with their propensity for eating human corpses.

Oh please. As if your Labradoodle wouldn't do the exact same thing if given half the chance.

> "*Varanus salvator*: Common Water Monitor," Animal Diversity Web, animaldiversity.org; "Malayan Water Monitor Lizard," Naturia, naturia.per.sg

When engineers working on a Brazilian dam in 2011 uncovered a rather . . . unusual animal, the zoological world was excited about the discovery of the new species *Atretochoana eiselti*. For a common name, the media quickly dubbed their pink, wrinkly, and throbbing discovery the "floppy snake," despite the fact that it was actually a caecilian (a type of legless amphibian). It was a pretty good name they came up with, but not as descriptive as it could possibly be. So they gave it another try with "manaconda," and then they just stopped beating around the bush and named the damn thing for what it resembles most in the world: the "penis snake." Finally, they found out that a desiccated, flaccid specimen of this very creature had been floating in a jar at a museum for the past 100 years.

> ❯ "'Penis Snake' Discovered in Brazil Is Actually a Rare Species of Amphibian," Mongabay, mongabay.com

But I suppose it's understandable that even the media would want to purge the idea of a disembodied cock monster from their collective memories at the earliest opportunity.

Caecilians (Latin for "blind ones") are legless, wormlike amphibians that live beneath the soil all over the globe. For something so simple-looking, the females are surprisingly generous when it comes to feeding their children. When her terrible little babies are conceived, they immediately start dining on her flesh inside the womb. And once they're out, depending on the species, they will sustain themselves by scraping off her skin with a variety of teeth, some spoon-like and others that resemble "grappling hooks."

> ❯ "Flesh-Eating Baby 'Worm' Feasts on Mom's Skin," *National Geographic*, nationalgeographic.com

Sadly, many species of caecilians are listed as endangered. Partly because of human encroachment, but mostly due to postpartum depression.

Alligator snapping turtles (*Macrochelys temminckii*) are far and away the most hazardous (non–mutant ninja) turtles, and are as good at instigating panic at lakes as sharks are at the beach. Native to the southeastern United States, the fear they inspire is definitely justified, as their powerful bites are perfectly capable of removing human appendages at will. Somehow one of these menaces got to Germany a few years ago and wound up in the Bavarian village of Irsee, where it introduced itself by severing the Achilles tendon of a young boy. The mayor responded by draining an entire lake, and offered a sizable cash reward for the turtle's capture.

❯"Alligator Snapping Turtle," *National Geographic*, nationalgeographic.com; "Vicious Bite: Dangerous Turtle At Large in Bavaria," Spiegel Online, spiegel.de

Obviously, a ban on skinny-dipping was immediately put in place, as no turtle can resist the lure of untethered schnitzel.

The Suriname toad has a surprisingly festive scientific name (*Pipa pipa*), considering it looks like a dead frog that's been run over by a cartoon steamroller. But the most troubling thing about Suriname toads has nothing to do with how they look, but rather the way they're born. Their tadpoles aren't released into the water to frolic like others of their ilk—they're nestled underneath the skin of their mothers' backs. And once they reach the "toadlet" stage, they burst forth in a way that would make Ridley Scott throw up in his mouth.

❯"Suriname Toad (*Pipa pipa*)," Wildscreen Arkive, arkive.org

So to all the mothers who complain that having kids ruined their looks, just be glad you didn't have chestburster babies.

The Mexican mole lizard (*Bipes biporus*) looks like a cross between an earthworm and a snake at first glance. Then the "mole" part becomes a bit clearer when you notice the stubby little arms on either side that it uses for tunneling around underneath the soil. The locals in Baja, California, are downright terrified of these tiny creatures, because legend has it they love to wait until an unsuspecting human squats down to relieve him- or herself, and then scurry right up the butthole to wreak havoc on the internal organs.

> *"Bipes biporus,"* Encyclopedia of Life, eol.org

That's probably not true at all. It's likely just as unfounded as that awful Richard Gere rumor. So he should really calm down, stop researching how to order Mexican mole lizards online, and just move on to the next entry.

The Chinese giant salamander (*Andrias davidianus*) looks like a 6-foot-long bowel movement with beady little eyes, and is the most humongous representative of its slimy kind. They live for more than fifty years and breathe entirely through their mottled, wrinkly skin. And to the shock of absolutely no one, they're considered a delicacy in Asia. A slightly smaller version, known as the hellbender, can be found in the eastern United States, from New York to Georgia. It also looks like a massive turd, but more like it came out of someone who suffers from a problem that causes blood in his stool.

> "Chinese Giant Salamander (*Andrias davidianus*)," Wildscreen Arkive, arkive.org

The moral of the story is: if you ever find yourself in rural West Virginia, don't order the "swamp chicken."

The green (or common) iguana (*Iguana iguana*) has long been a popular pet among the odd and the socially unacceptable alike. And while these reptiles can at times be quite dangerous, they do at least provide a good alternative for owners who might otherwise be kidnapping hitchhikers. However, women who keep iguanas as pets may find that sharing the same space with such an unusual creature can be a little more "exotic" than they bargained for. What I'm trying to say here is, iguanas are able to smell when human females are menstruating. And sometimes this makes them highly aggressive, and prone to attempt mating with their owners.

Hey, I'm not going to judge. Whatever an open-minded lady and a willing lizard choose to do in the privacy of their own home couldn't be any worse than what probably happens in Matthew McConaughey's basement on a regular basis.

❯ "Male Iguanas in Breeding Season and Human Females," Melissa Kaplan's Herp Care Collection, anapsid.org

---

In 2015, researchers in Ecuador stumbled across the "punk rocker frog" (*Pristimantis mutabilis*). Unique among all amphibians, these frogs can change the texture of their skin at will. They were given that anarchic nickname because of their ability to immediately transform from a regular-looking frog into one that's completely covered in a threatening array of spikes.

I get the "liberty spikes" reference, but wouldn't "heavy metal frogs" be more appropriate? There must be some story involving a young herpetologist and a bad experience backstage at a Mötley Crüe concert we're just not hearing about.

❯ "*Pristimantis mutabilis*: Scientists Discover Shape-Shifting Frog in Ecuador," Sci News, sci-news.com

The diminutive tiger keelback was long thought to be a non-venomous snake, until people realized that getting bitten by one of these Japanese snakes resulted in some nasty symptoms. One of which was dropping dead. What made things initially confusing was that their fangs, being in the back of their mouths instead of the front, weren't immediately visible. What's more, keelbacks don't actually have any venom of their own. What they do is kill poisonous toads, steal their toxins, and then store them in glands to add the lethal badness to their bites.

Apparently they're the only known snakes that do something like this, and scientists were thrilled to make such an amazing discovery. The toads, not so much.

❯"Snakes Eat Poisonous Toads and Steal Their Venom," *New Scientist*, newscientist.com

There are some animals in existence that can regenerate lost tissue, like how some lizards can grow back a lost tail and whatnot. But the Mexican axolotl salamander (*Ambystoma mexicanum*) is not only able to accomplish that, but it can also regrow a foot, its spine, and even portions of its brain should the need arise.

What kind of tragic lives do these things lead to make something like this a necessity? Is axolotl the ancient Aztec word for "f***ed"?

❯"Biology of Axolotls," Axolotls, axolotl.org

For a long time it was believed that Komodo dragons took down large prey, like pigs and deer, by infecting them with bacteria that the huge lizards cultivated inside their filthy, filthy mouths. Nope! It turns out to be not that complicated at all. It was recently revealed that Komodo dragons simply had good old-fashioned venom all along. Not to say that their oral hygiene isn't still atrocious. They have red saliva that helps a little with the lubrication, but it can still take up to twenty minutes to swallow a dead goat. And not long afterward, just like with every meal they consume, they vomit up the leftover, indigestible body parts in a tidy little package called a "gastric pellet" that emerges slathered in a vile-smelling mucous.

And as disgusting as that sounds, it's probably not quite as bad as that How It's Made *episode on haggis.*

❯"Here Be Dragons: The Mythic Bite of the Komodo," *Discover*, discovermagazine.com; "Feeding Habits of the Komodo Dragon," Komodo Dragons, komododragonfacts.com; "Ten Fierce Facts about Komodo Dragons," World Wildlife Fund, worldwidlife.org

The male Emei moustache toad (*Leptobrachium boringii*) indeed has a mustache, and it is indeed quite fancy. The fact that the word *boring* is in its scientific name is a travesty. Its dignified lip whiskers are actually spikes, and they aren't just for show. They're as hard as pencil tips and are used in flesh-rending duels with fellow toads during mating season.

❯"Hipster Toad Has Weaponised Moustache," *New Scientist*, newscientist.com

During these competitions the toads carry themselves with the utmost dignity. Yet there always seems to be one jackass who says something about a "mustache ride," ruining it for everyone.

Australian Fitzroy River turtles (*Rheodytes leukops*) are called "bum breathers" because they . . . ahem . . . breathe out of their asses. The process is actually called "cloacal respiration," but a pretty title in no way diminishes the distastefulness of what this reptile is up to. Which, to reiterate, is sucking air in through its anus (sorry, cloaca). Fitzroy turtles get up to 70 percent of their oxygen this way, and the ability to breathe from multiple orifices allows them to stay underwater for over a week before needing to rise to the surface and embarrass everyone around with their butthole wheezing.

> "Australia's Bum-Breathing Turtle Gets a Helping Hand," Ontario Turtle Conservation Centre, kawarthaturtle.org

As negligent as it would be to teach a turtle to smoke, you could probably make a lot of carnival money with a turtle that can blow rings from both ends.

Invasive brown tree snakes have basically taken over Guam, and their numbers have exploded to such an outrageous extent that the authorities have resorted to some pretty drastic measures. Like the time in 2013 when the government parachuted thousands of dead, poison-filled mice onto an Air Force base. One thing that makes this kind of desperation understandable is the fact that the snakes seem to have an affinity for attacking human babies in their cribs while they sleep.

Hopefully the situation improves soon, before the Air Force starts implementing the early stages of Operation Poison Baby Drop.

> "Two Thousand Mice Dropped on Guam by Parachute—to Kill Snakes," NBC News, nbcnews.com; "Risks to Infants on Guam from Bites of the Brown Tree Snake (*Boiga irregularis*)," by T.H. Fritts, M. Mccoid, and R. Haddock, *American Journal of Tropical Medicine and Hygiene* (1990), researchgate.net

Little devil poison frogs (*Oophaga sylvatica*) may have a name that suggests they're simply incorrigible yet adorable scamps (well, aside from the "poison" part), but they're fairly brutal when it comes to raising their young. A little devil mama frog is very attentive to her children's needs, however, and will go to great lengths to make sure her babies are well-fed after they've hatched—by fattening them up with the unhatched eggs out of her womb. They're unfertilized, at least, if that softens the horror.

❯ "*Oophaga sylvatica*," Encyclopedia of Life, eol.org

Sure! There would be nothing gross at all about cooking an omelet and then feeding it to a bunch of chicks, for instance. While you watched. Smiling. Remembering the good times you had with Clarice Starling while you were both on the hunt for Buffalo Bill.

In 2008 we found out that we were sharing the planet with something called the "vampire flying frog." The new species, discovered in the jungles of Vietnam, was named *Rhacophorus vampyrus*, and terrifying fangs are definitely part of the equation. But it's not the adults that have the fangs—it's the tadpoles. Because they begin life feasting on the unfertilized eggs that their mothers pump out specifically for that purpose. And the vampire fangs are believed to be implements used for slicing wide open the little containers that were almost their little baby brothers and sisters.

❯ "'Vampire Flying Frog' Found; Tadpoles Have Black Fangs," *National Geographic*, nationalgeographic.com

This information could have made Jon & Kate Plus 8 *a much more interesting show, knowing that at any time one of the sextuplets could have been devoured in a frenzy of ravenous toddlers.*

From all indications, it appears prairie rattlesnakes (*Crotalus viridis*) in South Dakota are gradually losing their rattles. Because announcing their presence with a loud warning noise only makes them a target for destruction when humans are around, evolution seems to be helping them out by making them quieter. Eventually, scientists believe, the fearsome snake's legendary rattle will degrade into complete uselessness.

So the next time you visit rattlesnake country, don't bother being on your guard for loud noises. Instead, be wary of the soft yet rapid thumping of an angry nub.

❯ "Some Rattlesnakes Losing Their Warning Rattle in S. Dakota," National Public Radio, npr.org

In 2014 researchers found disconcerting but conclusive proof that crocodiles can climb trees. This bad news wasn't based on just one observation made by some drunk scientist during a malarial fugue. Four crocodile species on three different continents were observed engaging in this arboreal behavior. And apparently they can get all the way up to the topmost branches, as well.

Clearly this is just the first stage. Are we going to allow this to happen until the day of the flying crocodiles is upon us?

❯ "Crikey! Crocodiles Can Climb Trees," Live Science, livescience.com

Both mugger crocodiles (*Crocodylus palustris*) in India and American alligators (*Alligator mississippiensis*) in our own backyard have been observed playing a particularly nasty trick. The overgrown lizards will pile sticks on their faces and lie partially submerged in the water. And when an unsuspecting stork or heron wanders by to collect some building materials, the beasts lurch out of the water and decimate the bird.

> ❯ "Tool Use in Crocodylians: Crocodiles and Alligators Use Sticks As Lures to Attract Waterbirds," *Scientific American*, scientificamerican.com

Scattered reports of alligators in Florida stockpiling squeaky toys and biscuits are troubling but remain unconfirmed.

There are certain frogs that refuse be satisfied

with the earthly limitations of hopping and so have decided to take flight. In fact, there are a ton of them. Some have evolved webbed feet that act like floppy parachutes, and others can actually splay those feet out to glide through the air like slimy paragliders. One of the largest of the airborne amphibians is the 4-inch Wallace's flying frog (*Rhacophorus nigropalmatus*), native to Malaysia and Borneo, which spends the majority of its life soaring, as majestically as is possible for a frog, from tree to tree.

Which makes camping in the area all the more annoying, since along with the mosquito repellant, the water purifier, and all the rest of the gear, you also have to pack a frogswatter.

❯ "Wallace's Flying Frog," *National Geographic*, nationalgeographic.com

There are a few lizards that can take to the air like scaly, repugnant birds on the featherless wing. There's actually an entire genus of them, called *Draco*, otherwise known as the flying dragons. Their "wings," disturbingly, are actually elongated ribs with skin connecting them to their forearms, along with flappy bits of skin on their necks to serve as stabilizers. They can't flap themselves along indefinitely, so they technically glide instead of fly. But they nonetheless are able to swoop for maximum distances of 200 feet.

❯ *"Draco volans*: Common Flying Dragon," Animal Diversity Web, animaldiversity.org; "Draco: Flying Lizards," Encyclopedia of Life, eol.org

The Flying Lizards also happens to be the name of an English experimental rock band known for their "avant-garde" and "free-improvising" musicianship. You tell me which one would be more disturbing to find on your significant other's coffee table.

Because I'm sure you were wondering, there is also a flying snake. There are five species of them in the genus *Chrysopelea*, and they actually slither their flattened bodies through the air. The aerodynamics involved have been of great interest to researchers over the years, and the fact that these serpents are actually maximizing their gliding potential, by controlling airflow via their hideous undulating, was only uncovered in the past few years.

Flying snakes are often described as being "mildly venomous," but a little goes a long way when you're dealing with a GODDAMN FLYING SNAKE.

❯ "Flying Snakes' Secret Revealed," Live Science, livescience.com

All female sea turtles lumber ashore to lay their eggs, and they lay a lot of them at a time. When hatching time comes, thousands upon thousands of unbearably cute babies spastically attempt to crawl their way to the water. However, various birds, crabs, and other predators turn their journey into a reptilian version of Omaha Beach. And once they do eventually reach the water, the carnage continues. It's probably best that you don't become too attached, because only an estimated one in 1,000–10,000 survives to adulthood.

> "Information about Sea Turtles: Threats to Sea Turtles," Sea Turtle Conservancy, conserveturtles.org

Which, admittedly, is better odds than most child actors get.

Amazon horned frogs (*Ceratophrys cornuta*) are often referred to as "Pac-Man frogs," due to a preposterously oversized mouth and an appetite to match. They're more than capable of wolfing down a rat whole, and have been known to accidentally burst themselves by gobbling prey that was far too large to fit inside their stomachs.

> "Amazon Horned Frog: *Ceratophrys cornuta,*" *National Geographic,* nationalgeographic.com

You can actually buy these at pet stores, by the way. Right there in the section marked "Lingering Childhood Trauma."

Horned frogs are plenty repulsive when they're fully grown adults, but they're arguably worse as tadpoles. While they're scooting along in the water waiting to grow legs, they're just as aggressively carnivorous as their parents. They'll happily gorge themselves on the tadpoles of other species, and if they should find themselves under attack, they're the only known vertebrate larvae that can scream. Even worse, scientists have described the sound as "metallic."

Using these animals would go a long way toward eliminating horseplay during biology class dissections, to be sure. In fact, the students might not ever speak again the entire rest of the year.

❯ "Frog Tadpoles 'Scream' Underwater Discover Scientists," BBC, bbc.com

Alligator attacks, fatal and otherwise, are on the rise in the southeastern United States. This alarming fact was brought to broad public attention by a recent tragedy at Florida's Disney World. Not to mention the incident where a fisherman found an alligator carrying around a human torso near Fort Lauderdale. With regard to that last one, as of this writing the victim has yet to be identified, and the closest human habitation is a retirement home.

❯ "Human-Alligator Encounters Rising in Southeast U.S.," *National Geographic*, nationalgeographic.com

So shifting your retirement plan toward Arizona is looking pretty good about now, eh?

Should you happen to be bitten by a Russell's pit viper and live to tell the tale, there's a 29 percent chance its venom will give you something called Sheehan's syndrome. This condition affects the pituitary gland, and what follows is a loss of sex drive and pubic hair. Next to go will be muscle tone for men, while women will lose their curves. Mental acuity may also degrade, and it's at this point that you might realize that you're basically going through puberty, only in reverse.

Which is only made worse when the emergency room nurses start to whisper and giggle amongst themselves, while a handsome doctor starts smacking you in the ass with a wound-up towel.

❯"The Deadly Russell Viper: How the Snake's Venom Affects Humans," *Indian Express*, indianexpress.com

The armadillo girdled lizard (*Cordylus cataphractus* or *Ouroborus cataphractus*) has a defense technique that sounds absolutely useless on paper: biting its own tail. But the plentiful spikes that line its entire body actually make it pretty darn effective in practice. The tail-biting maneuver essentially turns the lizard into an improvised wheel of pain that's more than enough to dissuade all but the most masochistic of pursuers. And if transforming itself into a shuriken doesn't work, their backup plan is to bite so hard their jaw breaks.

❯"Armadillo girdled lizard (*Cordylus cataphractus*)," Wildscreen Arkive, arkive.org; "Armadillo Lizard—Tough Desert Reptile," FactZoo, factzoo.com

And I assume if THAT doesn't work, they just crap themselves. It worked in prison for me that one time, so it should apply here just as well.

As spooky as reptiles can get, we can at least be thankful that none of them glows in the dark. Um . . . except for this weird-ass biofluorescent turtle we just found, I guess. We've known about hawksbill sea turtles (*Eretmochelys imbricata*) for practically forever, but it was only in 2015 that we discovered one that lit up like a neon Christmas tree when exposed to blue light. We still don't know whether it's due to algae or something that the shell does on its own.

And based on what I know about how police use blue lights to investigate crime scenes, let's hope these turtles aren't just covered in whale splooge.

❯ "Glowing Sea Turtle Is 1st Biofluorescent Reptile Ever Discovered," CBC, cbc.ca

---

Frogs aren't known for having an overabundance of pride,

and no species exemplifies this character deficiency more than the pied warty frog (*Theloderma asperum*). You can look for them in the wetlands of Asia, but you'd be lucky to find one. Because, like many creatures, this frog uses the art of camouflage to conceal itself from predators. Yet few go to the lengths of our warty friend, whose patterns and texture make it look exactly like crap. If they have even the slightest bit of embarrassment over their other common name, the "bird poop frog," they're not showing it.

I suppose you could say there's a certain dignity in being eternally disgusting, especially if you see any merit in the continuing popularity of the Kardashian family.

❯ "*Theloderma asperum*, a Member of Frogs and Toads (Order Anura)," iNaturalist, inaturalist.org

In order to deal with the complications of both genders being attached to unwieldy and cumbersome shells, most male turtles have developed unreasonably huge genitalia. And they're rather fond of whipping out their equipment at inappropriate moments, in an activity called "penis fanning." And should you ever consider keeping a male turtle as a pet, keep in mind that an extremely unpleasant but necessary task must be accomplished with regularity. And that would be cleaning its dick.

❯ "Terrifying Sex Organs of Male Turtles," *Scientific American*, scientificamerican.com

---

Admittedly, that's one hell of an excuse to get out of just about anything.

Rhinella proboscidea **are scrawny, plain-looking frogs** that are common in the Amazon Rainforest. There is really not much to say about them. Well, apart from the functional reproductive necrophilia. These frogs have a mating season that is so short and so intense that the males will pile on to the females in a frenzy, often causing the target of their ardor to drown. That's just fine, though—the male simply dry-humps the eggs right out of her corpse and fertilizes them where they lie.

❯ "Croakus Interruptus," *The Scientist*, the-scientist.com

In a way, it's kind of romantic. Wait a second. Oh God. No it isn't. Not at all.

It's not hard to imagine a constrictor slithering around the swamps of Florida, but Canada? However, the rubber boa (*Charina bottae*) is actually native to the great Northwest, and the species is so named because they indeed look just like partially deflated inner tubes. These boas are sometimes also called "two-headed snakes" due to the extreme knobbiness of their tails, which are often scarred from fighting off adult mice while the snake's actual head is busy eating their children.

And just to make things extra horrible for the mice, it's been theorized that some rubber boas will paint up their tails to look like clowns.

❯ "Rubber Boa," The Reptiles of British Columbia, bcreptiles.ca

There's no such thing as a venomous turtle, thank goodness, but some of them can be quite poisonous. To eat, that is. Seeing as how some species of box turtles include a variety of toxic mushrooms in their diet, making a meal out of one can prove not just trippy but fatal.

I guess it might not be all that surprising to learn that eating turtles can be dangerous. Especially with all these mutant ninja ones running around our sewers.

❯ "Box Turtle," Smithsonian National Zoological Park, nationalzoo.si.edu

When horned lizards ("horny toads" if you're nasty) find themselves cornered, they'll shoot blood from their eyes at an attacker. You might be aware of that. But what might be a little more surprising is that when members of the genus *Phrynosoma* get really pissed, they'll unleash an entire third of their blood supply into their harasser's face. And after eating a steady diet of venomous harvester ants, that can make for quite a spicy meatball.

Making them a handy accessory for PETA protesters, able to soak a rich old lady's fur coat to satisfaction while also fitting neatly into a back pocket or purse.

❯ "Horror Lizard Squirts Tears of Blood," *New Scientist*, newscientist.com

There are a number of invasive species that have taken up residence in the Sunshine State of Florida (alternately, "America's Wang"). But none has captured the public's imagination so much as the Burmese python (*Python bivittatus*). These immense, slithering constrictors have certainly found both the climate and topography to their liking, and eradication efforts will soon be an exercise in pointlessness. Because they're no longer the "giant snake swallows retired woman's prize schnauzer whole" local interest story anymore—current estimates put their numbers in the millions.

With alligator attacks on the rise and now a burgeoning python population, these are indeed dark times for nude camping enthusiasts.

❯ "The Snake That's Eating Florida," *New York Times*, nytimes.com

You know the term *crocodile tears*, which refers to when somebody cries like a baby but doesn't really mean it? It came from the legend that crocodiles weep while eating, but it turns out it may have some basis in reality. It doesn't relate to reptilian insincerity, however, but has everything to do with how crocodiles are gross. Research suggests that when crocodiles violently consume their meals (which can range from birds to fish to wildebeests to you), air gets forced through their sinus cavities, which mixes with the fluid in their tear ducts and results in bubbly, frothy tears.

❯ "No Faking It, Crocodile Tears Are Real," ScienceDaily, sciencedaily.com

There's still so much we have yet to learn about reptile sadness. For all we know they're overcome with shame whenever they tear some old lady's poodle to ribbons. Probably not, though.

African burrowing vipers (subfamily Atractaspidinae) are also known as, and I'm being dead serious here, "side-stabbing stiletto snakes." They have fangs that are so long that they actually do that ridiculous nickname justice. They protrude so outrageously that the snakes are able to shank you with them without even opening their mouths. And by no means are they "all stab and no squirt," meaning they pack so much venom that the glands that produce it account for 20 percent of their entire body length.

❯ "Side-Stabbing Stiletto Snakes," ScienceBlogs, scienceblogs.com

All that's pretty impressive, but what I really want to know is why they gave this snake the same nickname my dad used to use for his first wife?

We all know frogs can be poisonous, and have probably seen the particularly gaudy "poison arrow" versions that live in the Amazon. But in 2015 we found the first ones that are venomous. Meaning they have a delivery system, like a snake's fangs, to put their poison inside you. What the Greening's frog and the Bruno's casque-headed frog (both also from the Amazon, of course) do is bash you with the bony, toxin-filled spines on their heads.

> ❯ "First Known Venomous Frogs Use Their Heads As Weapons," Sci News, sci-news.com

Thus, combining the joys of toad-licking and heroin needles into one convenient package.

When the lizards known as long-tailed skinks

(*Mabuya longicaudata*) get tired of constantly having to fight off snakes seeking to steal their eggs, they have a rather unique solution to the problem—they eat the eggs themselves. The technical term for this unthinkable act is *whole-clutch filial cannibalism*, and it's a case of practicality taken to obscene extremes. Basically, if a skink becomes convinced that a marauding snake is going to win in the end anyway, it reckons, "Hey, I might as well eat all these yummy lizard omelets myself."

But before you condemn these animals out of hand, be sure to consider the old adage, "Never judge someone until after you've walked a mile in their baby-cannibalizing shoes."

> ❯ "Predation Risk of Whole-Clutch Filial Cannibalism in a Tropical Skink with Maternal Care," by W. Huang, *Behavioral Ecology* (2008), oxfordjournals.org

Getting eaten by a snake would be horrible under any circumstances, but at least most species have the common decency to either poison or strangle you to death beforehand. However, not all snakes are so merciful. A few don't bother with any of the foreplay whatsoever, and simply swallow prey whole while it's very much alive and fully aware of what's going on. Occasionally it's a matter of the snakes not wanting to exert themselves unnecessarily with easy prey (like baby rabbits). But there's no "occasionally" as far as the Eurasian grass snake is concerned; it loves to consume each and every hapless thing it catches alive and wriggling.

> ❯ "Grass Snake (*Natrix natrix*)," Wildscreen Arkive, arkive.org

That's disgusting. Everyone knows baby rabbits taste better boiled.

Ilha de Queimada Grande is a small land mass off the coast of Brazil with a charming nickname: Snake Island. The place is so dense with venomous vipers (some estimate five snakes per square meter) that the Brazilian navy won't allow people to visit. The serpent infestation happened naturally, when the island separated from the mainland 11,000 years ago. And since that time, the snakes' venom has evolved to become five times as deadly as any of their counterparts' back on the mainland.

> ❯ "This Terrifying Brazilian Island Has the Highest Concentration of Venomous Snakes Anywhere in the World," *Smithsonian,* smithsonianmag.com

If Gilligan and the rest of those idiots had landed on this particular island, it would definitely have made for a much more watchable show.

You might have heard of the religious sect that includes snake handling in their repertoire. Somehow the extreme Pentecostals of the "Holiness Movement" never reconsidered the wisdom in this endeavor after the man who popularized the activity, George Went Hensley, ended a service by rubbing his face with a rattlesnake. After which the snake responded by promptly killing Mr. Hensley in the normal manner that rattlesnakes do.

Which is why if you want the cult you've started to have any staying power at all, you probably shouldn't require every member to prove his faith through the use of cobra suppositories.

> *Taking Up Serpents: Snake Handlers of Eastern Kentucky* by David L. Kimbrough

Even if you cut the head off a venomous snake, you're still not safe from its wrath. These snakes' reflexive ability to bite can remain for hours after they're dead. Just ask the guy from central Washington, who dispatched a rattlesnake on his property by decapitating it with a shovel. After reveling for a moment in his victory over the forces of nature, he reached down to dispose of the corpse. Whereupon the rattler's disembodied head performed a backflip and sank its fangs directly into the man's approaching hand.

> "Bodyless Rattlesnake Head Bites Man," Wildlife Management Pro, wildlifemanagementpro.com; "Can a Severed Snake Head Still Kill? It's Possible," Live Science, livescience.com

That must have been both painful and humiliating, but the most embarrassing part had to be when the rattle started shaking to the tune of Rick Astley's "Never Gonna Give You Up."

There was one incident, during the Pacific campaign of WWII, that just goes to show that getting killed or taken prisoner by the enemy isn't necessarily the worst thing that can happen in war. When Japanese troops in Burma were retreating after getting the worst of it in the Battle of Ramree Island, it's believed hundreds of the fleeing soldiers were torn apart and devoured by crocodiles.

> ❯ "Worst Ever Crocodile Attack," Wild World, iberianature.com

Which is why many crocodiles today refer to the brave men and women who served their countries during that period in history as "The Greatest-Tasting Generation."

Keeping a lizard is usually a relatively reasonable thing to do, but not when it's 6 feet long and has claws like a velociraptor. To further illustrate this generally accepted truism, when police searched the home of a forty-two-year-old reptile enthusiast in Newark, Delaware, back in 2002, the first thing they noticed was that the man had passed away. Actually, maybe that was the second thing they noticed, since he was surrounded by no fewer than seven Nile monitor lizards (*Varanus niloticus*), feasting upon his remains.

Investigators couldn't be sure if the lizards had actually killed the man, as the lizards had been in the city long enough to know that the smart move was to take advantage of their right to remain silent.

❯ "Lure of the Exotic Stirs Trouble in the Animal Kingdom," *New York Times*, nytimes.com

CHAPTER 8

Wrathful Weather and Other Nefarious Natural Phenomena

Whether you're on top of an earthquake fault line, in the middle of a hurricane corridor, or stuck on a remote island with a simmering volcano in the middle, no matter where you go there's a natural phenomenon just waiting to end you. Sometimes disasters can even team up in various combinations of earth, wind, water, and/or fire to more thoroughly ensure your destruction. And while you might relegate what happened in the Sharknado movies (which may be up to part six by the time you're reading this) to the realm of fictional silliness, keep in mind that frognados have happened. Jellyfish-nados too. There's a reason why early religions focused so much on trying to convince the heavens not to hammer them with natural calamities. And that's because when the giant waves come rolling in or a yawning crater swallows your home, there's not a damn thing mankind can really do about it. So we might as well just accept the fact that we're not in charge in the slightest, relax, and admire the spectacles, like . . .

"Non-aqueous rain" refers to the very real phenomenon where the skies open up and rain down not water but inscrutable things like fish and frogs. Or jellyfish. Or spiders. Or sometimes chunks of meat. As much as it sounds like some sort of "wrath of God" scenario, the explanation is likely much less apocalyptic. And I say "likely" because we don't have any concrete explanation as to why it occurs. Heck, for all we know it could be the act of a vengeful, frog-hating deity. But the likeliest explanation is that waterspouts periodically suck up creatures from faraway waters, carry them up into the sky, and deposit them onto the heads of bewildered and terrified humans. But what about the falling meat? Thankfully, that one has actually been explained, and it involves vomiting vultures.

❯"Can It Really Rain Cats and Dogs?" *Farmers' Almanac*, farmersalmanac.com; "The Great Kentucky Meat Shower Mystery Unwound by Projectile Vulture Vomit," *Scientific American*, scientificamerican.com

Which still should be more than enough trauma to make the average TV weatherman give up everything to wander the streets in a robe carrying a handmade "THE END IS NIGH" sign.

Venezuela is home to the most electric place on Earth. And considering the state of their economy, it obviously has nothing to do with the power grid in Caracas. At precisely the small geographical spot where the Catatumbo River meets Lake Maracaibo, an average of 260 storm days occur every year. And any one of them can potentially include thousands of lightning strikes in a single hour. While theories range from an overabundance of uranium in the bedrock to methane in the air produced by nearby oil fields, we still have no proof of why "Catatumbo lightning" is so prolific.

❯"The Most Electric Place on Earth," BBC, bbc.com

Unless we've finally found the place where Thor disappears to in order to masturbate.

A "brinicle" is something along the lines of an underwater icicle, but it's way more devastating than the ones hanging from your rain gutters—at least for any hapless life forms that might find themselves directly beneath one. Also referred to by some as "the finger of death," a brinicle is what happens when frozen saltwater falls from the sea ice and forms icy tendrils. Once one of these tendrils touches the bottom, it spreads out and acts like a freeze ray from a comic book supervillain's arsenal, immediately condemning everything it comes in contact with to a sub-zero-degree doom.

First the Titanic, and now this? When are people going to wake up and demand that the president start launching cruise missiles at icebergs? Or as I call them, "glacial insurgents."

> "'Brinicle' Ice Finger of Death Filmed in Antarctic," BBC, bbc.com

Scientists still don't know exactly what ball lightning is, and until the 1960s the phenomenon of floating orbs of UFO-like electricity that pass through walls like ghosts was considered to be nothing more than an urban myth. One person who wouldn't have agreed with that assessment was Georg Richmann, a pioneering electricity researcher who was zapped to death by one in 1753. Or the hundreds of pigs that were instantly fried on a farm in China in 2014.

> "Ball Lightning: A Shocking Scientific Mystery," *National Geographic*, nationalgeographic.com; "Instant Hog Roast: 170 Pigs Struck by Rare 'Ball of Lightning,'" *Metro*, metro.co.uk

If the folks at Cracker Barrel could somehow harness this power, IHOP and Denny's would go out of business in a week.

"Dirty thunderstorm" is not an expression that refers to a wantonly filthy sex act but is instead a term that describes an actual meteorological phenomenon. It is pretty hardcore, nonetheless. It's what you call it when lightning bolts start firing out of a cloud of ash that has just arisen from the fiery, gaping maw of an erupting volcano.

A "gaping volcano" sounds like it might be pretty dirty, though, so you should probably avoid using that one in mixed company.

❯ "Mount Etna Erupted for the First Time in Two Years—and Something Incredible Happened," *Daily Mirror*, mirror.co.uk

---

The Potomac River is famous for its proximity to Washington, DC, and also for drowning lots of people who try to swim in it. The culprit, it seems, is a deceptively placid appearance that belies a powerful undercurrent that frequently pulls swimmers to their watery doom. After the National Park Service got sick of fishing out corpses, a campaign was put in place to warn incautious tubers and doggy paddlers that "If you enter the river, you will die."

❯ "'If You Enter the River, You Will Die,'" National Parks Traveler, nationalparkstraveler.com

Alternately, both Democrat and Republican officials are constantly trying to convince each other that the waters are perfectly safe, and definitely where they should spend their next vacation.

The mammatus (Latin for "mammary") cloud is meteorological event in which sagging pouches of air and water droplets form in the wake of a retreating storm. The collection of globular "udders" can measure around a half mile across, and although each one is composed of liquid and ice, they aren't really clouds, per se. But you're probably not going to care about details like that when you walk out the door and see the entire sky covered in saggy boobs.

Which reminds me of a nightmare I had, which my psychiatrist said had something to do with the time I walked in on my grandmother in the shower.

> "Clouds That Look Like Breasts," BBC News, bbc.co.uk

The freezing temperatures and sudden snowfalls in Finnish Lapland can make for some pretty trippy-looking visuals. Like when snow and ice attach themselves to trees so suddenly that they become entirely coated, causing the upper parts to bend ever so slightly, making the landscape look like it's covered in giant, floppy dicks.

Which must be a real treat for the eyes when spring rolls around, and the melting snow causes the entire area to look like an army of unconscious giants suffering from the late stages of ice gonorrhea.

> "Sentinels of the Arctic," NASA, nasa.gov

Tornadoes aren't made of just wind. They can be filled with dust, snow, Kansan farmhouses, nervous cows . . . what have you. One thing a tornado can also contain and distribute is fire. Tornados born from flame aren't as big as their better-known counterparts, but they don't need to be. They arise when an outdoor conflagration superheats the surrounding air, and can cause a run-of-the-mill wildfire to erupt in a 100-foot-high maelstrom of destruction.

The great thing about a fire tornado, though? You can poke a stick outside the shelter hatch to make "disaster s'mores."

> "How Fire Tornadoes Form," The Weather Channel, weather.com

Penitentes are phenomena that occur at high altitudes where there's a lot of snow but little in the way of humidity. Due to the unusual way evaporation occurs, an entire area can turn into a field filled with pointy spikes that can reach as high as 16 feet up in the air. Their name comes from the Spanish word for "penitent."

> "Nature Blows My Mind! The Strange Snow Formations Called Penitentes," Treehugger, treehugger.com

Which might be a reference to how sorry your ass will be if you're forced to land there in your parachute.

People often associate rainy weather with an increased suicide rate, but it turns out sunshine may make you more prone to killing yourself. Experts believe that the way sunlight affects serotonin, a chemical that can create feelings of happiness in the human brain, may have something to do with it. But while long periods of sunny weather do see fewer suicides than during crappy weather, for some reason it's when there are short bursts of sunshine in between periods of rain that a spike in suicides occurs.

❯"Curious Link Found Between Sunshine and Suicide Rates," *Tech Times*, techtimes.com

It's possible that the results could have been skewed if these studies took place in Illinois, at the start of spring training for the Chicago Cubs.

The phenomenon known as a "limnic eruption" has been observed only twice in human history. It's what happens when a lake, straight out of the blue, starts pumping out large amounts of carbon dioxide from a magma chamber that lies beneath. When this happens, a spooky white mist forms on the surface of the water. And when that mist creeps from the lake onto shore, and then makes contact with a human settlement, the results can be spectacularly dire. The event that occurred in 1986, near Lake Nyos in Cameroon, ended the lives of 1,800 people overnight. There are only three known lakes in the world where this sort of disaster can happen, and two of them are in Cameroon.

❯"Rwanda Harnesses Volcanic Gases From Depths of Lake Kivu," *Guardian*, theguardian.com

In other news, Cameroon probably has some wonderfully affordable vacation packages available for honeymooners on a budget.

A "derecho" is a type of windstorm that causes widespread "straight-line" damage. Which basically means that while a normal storm can wreak havoc in an area that's 1–2 miles wide and a few miles long, derechos "can produce damage swaths tens of miles wide and at least 250 miles long." The one that hit the mid-Atlantic and midwestern United States in 2012 is considered one of the most destructive weather events to ever occur in North America.

So basically, don't say the word derecho around a TV weatherman, unless you're fully prepared to deal with his sudden and massive erection.

❯"Derecho: The Science Behind Widespread Damaging Thunderstorm Winds," The Weather Channel, weather.com

In 1902, on the Caribbean island of Martinique, the worst volcano disaster in history claimed tens of thousands of lives. But the actual explosion may not have been the worst part. Before that apocalyptic event even occurred, the vibrations caused by the impending eruption terrified the local animal population, sending down hordes of venomous snakes, poisonous insects, and other unpleasantness from the mountains and into populated areas.

❯"Three Minutes of Horror When 30,000 Perished," *Guardian*, theguardian.com

Visitors to the island today can see some of the volcano's victims, frozen in time like the ash statues of Pompeii, still swatting away snakes and bugs while running from lava and wondering what the hell they did to deserve all this.

Quicksand used to be a go-to plot device in old movies and TV shows, but the reality is that people don't really sink the way they do in fictional portrayals. While it's entirely possible to get stuck for a while, you're highly unlikely to die from quicksand. Well, unless the quicksand in question is next to the ocean. And the tide is coming in. And the water level rises before you can extricate yourself. And nobody can hear your panicked screams in time.

Sharks often refer to this scenario as "surf lollipops."

> "Can Quicksand Really Suck You to Your Death?" BBC, bbc.com

A sudden spring snowstorm took South Dakota by surprise in 2013 as an unseasonable storm system sent icy winds tearing across the Midwest. The unusually cold weather caused all sorts of annoyances for the residents of Sioux Falls, including road closures, school cancellation, and the corpses of frozen turkey vultures raining down from the sky.

> "South Dakota Turkey Vultures: Storm Causes Frozen Birds to Rain from the Sky," *Huffington Post*, huffingtonpost.com

It just goes to show how inconsiderate turkey vultures are that they didn't do this on Thanksgiving.

Hail can be a real nuisance sometimes, denting cars and cracking windows. But you probably wouldn't want to complain about stuff like that to anyone who lived in Gopalganj, Bangladesh, in 1986. Because that was the year when ninety-two people were killed during a hailstorm that sent down giant balls of ice weighing over 2 pounds apiece.

The fact that a few entrepreneurs used the materials at hand to sell commemorative popsicles after the tragedy was judged to be in poor taste.

> "World: Heaviest Hailstone," Arizona State University, asu.edu

At the time of this writing a titanic rogue iceberg called B09B has taken the lives of 150,000 penguins. The gargantuan formation, which is the size of the entire city of Rome, became lodged in an Antarctic bay that a large colony of Adélie penguins (remember those degenerates?) call home. The penguins must now travel seventy miles to find food—an untenable situation that scientists believe will cause the birds to be completely wiped out in a matter of years.

This is indeed quite worrisome, yet it just may be the impetus these penguins need to finally get off their asses and fly like a normal goddamn bird.

> "150,000 Penguins Killed after Colossal Iceberg in Antarctica Leaves Colony Landlocked," *Independent*, independent.co.uk

Alberta, Canada's Lake Abraham in winter becomes replete with beautiful, jewel-like bubbles floating just underneath the surface. Looking down on the lake from the ice above is like peering through a window into a mystical fantasy universe. But unfortunately those bubbles are filled with methane, the result of the bacterial decomposition of dead things at the bottom of the lake. And should there be an open flame nearby when one of these bubbles pops, the experience will quickly transform into a not-so-magical case of third-degree burns.

❯ "Stunning Bubbles Frozen under Lake Abraham," *Smithsonian*, smithsonianmag.com

But you might want to try coming up with a more believable excuse when you're trying to convince emergency room staff that you weren't actually trying to light your farts on fire.

As awesome and magnificent as volcanoes are, you'll probably want to steer your kids away from studying them for a living. Out of a pool of only 200–300 volcanologists worldwide, twenty-three of them have been burned to a crisp over the past twenty years. But it's not just the lava that can kill you. There are also the myriad of poisonous gases and the superheated rocks whizzing around to worry about. The upside, at least, is that a death caused by volcano will most certainly be quick.

❯ "Study of Volcanoes a High-Risk Venture," *Pittsburgh Post Gazette*, old.post-gazette.com

But what a way to go, right? What a nasty, dreadful, unspeakably awful way to go.

Haboob is the term for a biblically huge wall of dust that can reduce visibility to zero, reach a height of 5,000 feet, and stretch as far as 100 miles wide. The term is Arabic in origin, and is usually used to describe the massive dust storms that sweep across the Sudan. The bigger ones can completely block out the sun and last for days.

The term has become popular among American weathermen recently, more than likely because it's so fun to say "boob" on live television.

❯"Arizona Monsoon: What Is a Haboob?" ABC 15 Arizona, abc15.com

But we should be thankful that there are at least a few people out there with the cojones to study volcanoes. Because maybe we'll one day understand why Mother Nature felt that something called a "supervolcano" was necessary. Also why there are several of them, waiting patiently to erupt and potentially bring about the end of all life on Earth.

❯"Supervolcanoes That Could Destroy Humanity 'May Explode Sooner Than Scientists Thought,'" _Independent_, independent.co.uk

But don't worry too much. I'm sure there's a Mayan calendar somewhere that will tell us all when it's time to board Halley's Comet and take a ride to a much shinier, happier planet.

A bog is not a swamp. The main difference is that bogs have poor soil quality but a lot of peat. They're acidic, waterlogged, and arguably even grosser than swamps. Especially when people toss their stray corpses in, which is something that happened with fair frequency in the ancient world. But what's special about throwing a body in a bog is, due to the unique composition of the water, soil, and peat, it turns dead people into mummies. And not just any mummies, but the most well-preserved (and surreally horrific) that history has to offer.

❯"World's Oldest Bog Body Hints at Violent Past," BBC News, bbc.com

Any experienced fisherman will probably tell you that bog fishing can be risky. In addition to life preservers and a reliable light source, it's always wise to bring along some stale haggis to appease the Scottish ghosts.

In 2001 the southern Indian state of Kerala was hit by a monsoon containing a large amount of a substance suspected to be red dust. Whatever it was, it caused an effect that made it appear as if it was raining blood. Obviously, people freaked out. One physicist, after examining samples of the rain, added to people's dismay when he declared that the substance was not in fact dust or sand, but instead something with "a clear biological appearance."

❯"Who What Why: What Is Blood Rain?" BBC News, bbc.com

What the hell does that mean? That is, shouldn't a "physicist" who knows that much about meteorology and biology be like, emperor of the world or something?

Sand and/or dust carried in the atmosphere from faraway places can have a similar effect on snow. Like the time some dust from Africa made it all the way to Russia and created a multicolored snowstorm that sparked widespread hyperventilating. And when volcanic ash occasionally finds its way into a storm, an ominous black snowfall can result, causing much gnashing of teeth.

And lo, the Lord did curse the unwashed of the region, "May your toboggans grow besotted, and your snowmen be as soot."

❯"Multicolored Snow in Russia? No Worries, Officials Say," *New York Times*, nytimes.com; *The Alaska Almanac: Facts about Alaska* by Nancy Gates

In addition to all the water, hail, and frogs that are constantly raining down from the sky, there are also 40,000 tons of space dust that make planetfall each and every year. Yet for some reason scientists say the Earth is actually losing mass by very small increments. Again, there are plenty of theories, but no solid reason not to worry about the situation future generations may face in about, say, a trillion years or so.

❯"Who, What, Why: Is the Earth Getting Lighter?" BBC News, bbc.com

Sure, that's a long way off. But I'm sure our descendants will appreciate any advantage we can provide against the tyranny of the galactic cybernetic squidlords.

The Inga Rapids of the Congo River are considered the planet's worst place to be if you should happen to be in a canoe. Described as "a 50-mile section of waterfalls, whirlpools, and kayak-eating hydraulics," and as "Earth's version of a fire hose," the ridiculously fast-traveling whitewater can produce 40-foot waves and has devoured more than its fair share of adventure seekers.

Note to budget-minded travelers: simply by camping downstream on the Congo River, one may easily pay the cost of one's African vacation by collecting and reselling all the expensive Gore-Tex that washes up on shore.

❯"Adventurers of the Year: The Kayaker: Steve Fisher," *National Geographic*, nationalgeographic.com; "Congo: The Grand Inga Rapids," Paddling Life, paddlinglife.net

The most powerful tornado ever recorded on Earth happened in "The Sooner State" of Oklahoma.

Meteorologists named the twister of all twisters "El Reno," which is Spanish for "The Reindeer." Okay, whatever. At any rate, this particular tornado earned an easy EF-5 rating (probably because an EF-6 exists only in the theories of madmen), sent 300 mph winds blasting across the landscape, and stretched an incredible 2.6 miles wide.

Let's just say if Dorothy from The Wizard of Oz *got caught up in this thing, the coroner would have needed weeks to track down all the fragments from the viscera dispersal.*

❯"Deadly El Reno, Okla. Tornado Was Widest Ever Measured on Earth, Had Nearly 300 mph Winds," *Washington Post*, washingtonpost.com

Dominica, a tiny island country in the Caribbean

(not to be confused with the Dominican Republic), is home to a lake that boils. As in, it bubbles and everything. Because of an abundance of volcanic gases, the water around the edges is a consistent 180–197 degrees Fahrenheit, and the exact temperature of the center (where the bubbling occurs) is unknown. Let's just say it's plenty hot.

Which means if the coastal waters have a decent lobster population, Dominica just might be my next vacation destination.

> "Dominica's Hot Water," A Virtual Dominica, avirtualdominica.com

Megacryometeor is the fancy word for "monstrous chunk of ice that falls out of the sky without warning." It has nothing to do with the frozen blocks of turds that airplanes jettison out onto an unsuspecting populace from time to time. There are doubts as to whether or not the phenomenon is weather related, but the truth is we simply don't know. What has been confirmed, however, is that they drop all over the world, and the largest one ever found was 440 pounds.

> "Huge Chunks of Ice Fall from the Sky," WeatherImagery, weatherimagery.com

If this doesn't turn out to be weather, it has government conspiracy written all over it. Extraterrestrial piss glaciers are real!

In 2013, Tropical Cyclone Oswald churned up so much sea foam that it turned some Australian coastal cities into the world's largest bubble bath. Rolling over vehicles and beachside stores like a whimsical tsunami, the foam created mass confusion and served as a sarcastic cherry on the cake of devastation left in the cyclone's wake. Prime Minister Julia Gillard was quoted expressing the nation's sadness by saying the "wild weather had broken a lot of hearts."

The Prime Minister may have been confusing the situation with an ongoing sex scandal, which coincidentally involved someone named "Bubbles."

❯"Australia Floods: Sunshine and Gold Coast Covered in 'Sea Foam,'" Yahoo News, uk.news.yahoo.com

In case you're wondering what the difference is between a cyclone, a typhoon, and a hurricane—there is none. Those are just different terms for the same thing, and they're used according to the part of the world where they occur. As far as cyclones go, the deadliest one happened in Bangladesh in 1970, killing a staggering 300,000–500,000 people.

❯"Typhoon? Hurricane? Cyclone? Here's the Difference," CBS News, cbsnews.com; "The Storm That Killed 300,000," The Weather Channel, weather.com

300,000–500,000? You know the situation's pretty dire when the margin for error is the entire population of Fresno.

Typhoons have a pretty violent rap sheet. Possibly the scariest was Super Typhoon Nancy, which battered Japan in 1961. Nancy's wind speeds were clocked at 215 mph, which were the fastest ever recorded. Well, until 2013, that is, when Super Typhoon Yolanda turned the Philippines into a smoldering scrapyard.

❯"Typhoon Haiyan/ Yolanda Strongest Storm on Earth?" AccuWeather, accuweather.com

Doesn't it seem just a little insensitive that all these life-ruining weather events sound like female professional wrestlers?

Lake Kivu in Africa has been described as a "ticking time bomb" because of the massive amounts of carbon dioxide and methane that lie beneath its surface. If released, the gases in the lake, which borders the Democratic Republic of the Congo and Rwanda, could eradicate the surrounding human population within a matter of hours. The government of Rwanda just recently installed a power plant to make use of the untapped energy resource, and we can only hope their safety measures are up to snuff to avoid an explosion of biblical proportions.

But even in a worst-case scenario, at least the long-suffering gorillas will be able to watch from up on their mountain and enjoy a brief moment of schadenfreude.

❯"Rwanda Harnesses Energy from Exploding Lake," NBC News, nbcnews.com; "Rwanda Inaugurates 26 MW Plant Using Methane from Lake Kivu," Reuters, af.reuters.com

The largest tornado to ever touch down happened in Oklahoma, which makes sense. What's harder to accept is that it was 2.6 miles across. Forty-one counties were affected by the EF-5 class twister (the highest category possible, obviously) and the governor was forced to declare a state of emergency less than two weeks after another devastating tornado famously ripped through the town of Moore.

❯ "El Reno tornado, at 2.6 miles across, was widest on record," NBC News, usnews.nbcnews.com

Prompting countries from around the world to donate surplus duct tape and baling wire to reassemble all the obliterated trailer parks.

Most lightning strikes are technically referred to as "negative" lightning, meaning they involve a transfer of negative charge from the cloud to the ground. However, 5 percent of strikes are "positive." And the reason you should care about all of that boring crap is because "positive" lightning strikes are not only up to 10 times stronger than the regular type, but they can also zap down from the heavens in the middle of a cloudless sky.

❯ "The Positive and Negative Side of Lightning," National Weather Service, srh.noaa.gov

See, God doesn't hate you; it's just science! But maybe both!

In 2013, when China experienced its worst heat wave in 140 years, things got so hot that people cooked meals on manhole covers and cars started exploding. Shanghai hit its all-time high temperature of over 104 degrees Fahrenheit, which may not sound like much if you live in Palm Springs, California, but it was enough to make people worry that their cell phones would turn into grenades.

❯ "China Endures Worst Heat Wave in 140 Years," *USA Today*, usatoday.com

I have no idea why they complained so much. Some people would kill for a chance to eat sewer quiche.

Due to volcanic activity, there are areas on Japan's Izu Islands that boast the highest concentration of poisonous gases in the world. But despite the islands having enough sulfur in the air to give Hell a run for its money, adventure seekers frequently visit to engage in an activity called "gas mask tourism." And if you should happen to show up completely unprepared, that's just fine, since the gift shops reportedly have an ample supply of HAZMAT gear. There's an image floating around the Internet of a decades-old wedding that took place on the Izu Islands where the bride, groom, and guests were wearing masks.

Hopefully it's legit, since having that many creepy fetishists in one place is entirely unacceptable outside of Brony conventions.

❯ "Gas Mask Tourism on the Izu Islands," Atlas Obscura, atlasobscura.com

In 2009 a dust storm in Sydney, Australia, brought forth a massive amount of red, iron-rich particles that had been kicked up from deep in the Outback. Once the overwhelming wave of particles reached the continent's most populous city, it rapidly covered everything in sight and made the entirety of the landscape look as if it had been replaced by the surface of Mars (or at least the movie poster for *Apocalypse Now*).

One would assume the citizenry reacted to the event in the same manner Australians respond to everything else: by getting drunk and babbling gibberish.

> "Sydney Turns Red: Dust Storm Blankets City," *Sydney Morning Herald*, smh.com.au

> "Leola Records 12 Degree Temperature Drop in 10 Minutes," Dakotafire, dakotafire.net

For some reason or another South Dakota is prone to wildly drastic temperature swings. Twelve-degree drops in the space of ten minutes and 18-degree drops in an hour aren't unheard of. And the record for this weirdness happened in the tiny town of Spearfish, where thermometers shot up 49 degrees in the space of only two minutes.

It's hard to prepare for something like that, but it just goes to show how right my grandmother was about the importance of layering.

There is such a thing as "ice tsunamis." While the regular kind can sneak up and take you by surprise, tidal waves made out of snow and chunks of ice take their time, creeping inexorably forward and destroying everything in their path like reverse-lava, or a much more sanitary version of *The Blob*. This type of tsunami happens with some regularity in Minnesota, when wind blows frozen ice off the lakes and onto shore.

When various citizens were queried as to how they felt about the situation, the universal response was "yah."

> "'Ice Tsunamis' Sweep Into Homes," CNN, cnn.com

Not every tornado is a feast for the eyes like the special effects extravaganzas in *Twister*. Sometimes they're completely invisible. Thunderstorms and heavy rains can obscure their presence, and even trained meteorologists might not have any idea what's about to come. And all those fancy Doppler radars won't help them either.

> "Invisible Storms: Rain-Wrapped Tornadoes Strike Florida," Live Science, livescience.com

I realize how preposterously insane it must sound to hear someone suggesting that weathermen can occasionally be wrong. But as risky as this entry is, I stand by my research.

When Indonesia's Mount Tambora erupted in 1815, the sudden blast was directly responsible for 92,000 deaths. That's hard enough to wrap your head around, but the immediate effects of the explosion were just the beginning. The amount of ash sent into the atmosphere was so immense that it caused persistently cold weather worldwide, resulting in what historians refer to as "The Year Without a Summer."

So all it would take to get Al Gore to stop bellowing about global warming is a worldwide cataclysm involving multiple volcanic doomsday scenarios? Seems like a fair tradeoff.

❯ "The Epic Volcano Eruption That Led to the 'Year Without a Summer,'" *Washington Post*, washingtonpost.com

❯ "Gateway to Hell: Turkmenistan Crater Has Been Burning for More Than 40 Years," *New York Daily News*, nydailynews.com

Turkmenistan's "Door to Hell" is a vast crater filled with methane. Back in 1971 the Soviets thought it would be a great place to set up a drilling rig, but when the apparatus they built was swallowed whole by the crater (which also caused it to get bigger) not long after they built it, they then decided it might be smart to burn off all that methane so the villages nearby wouldn't be blown to smithereens. Forty-five years later, it's still burning, filled with boiling mud and plenty of methane to spare.

Those must be some seriously exhausted villagers, because forty-five years is a long time to be nervous.

During WWI, thanks to a record-breaking amount of snowfall in the Tyrolean Alps (combined with a few well-placed manmade explosions), avalanches killed somewhere around 10,000 soldiers over the course of just a few days. Although this incident was likely unintentional, it may have led to the bright idea that avalanches could be a devastating weapon of war.

> "Soldiers Perish in Avalanche As World War I Rages," The History Channel, history.com

Allegedly when Hannibal tried something similar during his Alps crossing with elephants, the results were hilarious yet disappointing.

Ten thousand casualties from a single avalanche sounds very impressive, right up until you hear about the one that happened in Peru in 1970. An offshore earthquake triggered that one, and it obliterated an entire town of 25,000 people on a Sunday, when most of them were watching the World Cup game that was on at the time.

Which only goes to prove yet again what we should have admitted long ago: God hates soccer.

> "Yungay 1970–2009: Remembering the Tragedy of the Earthquake," *Andean Air Mail & Peruvian Times*, peruviantimes.com

"The Super Outbreak" is how meteorologists describe what happened in 1974 to the Midwest, Lower Mississippi Valley, and southeastern portion of the United States—when 148 tornadoes landed in the space of eighteen hours. It wouldn't have been so bad if they were merely the kind that knocks over a few plastic flamingos in a trailer park, but a whopping thirty of them were either F4- or F5-category mega twisters.

Finally convincing many residents who had foolishly constructed their doublewides out of straw and wood to finally make the switch to reinforced brick.

❯"Looking Back at the April 3–4, 1974 Super Outbreak," U. S. Tornadoes, ustornadoes.com

Of course we can't leave out earthquakes in a compilation like this, so let's go ahead and kick things off with the biggest. The earthquake that sucker-punched Valdivia, Chile, in 1960 measured 9.5 on the logarithmic magnitude scale. That's the equivalent of 20,000 atomic bomb blasts of the sort that decimated Hiroshima.

Yet despite all the "No Quakes" protesters who've been camping in front of the White House for years, there's still been no legislation preventing the spread of seismic injustice.

❯"Seismology: The Biggest One," *Nature*, nature.com

And if you're looking for spectacular death tolls, you really can't beat earthquakes. Sure, there may have been seismic events with higher numbers on the Richter scale than the quake that flattened Shanxi, China, back in the bygone year of 1556. But none of them snuffed out an estimated 830,000 souls. For reference, that's about 150,000 more people than the entire population of Detroit.

But since it will be a couple months before you read this, let's just say 300,000 more people than the entire population of Detroit.

> "Deadliest Earthquake in History Rocks China," The History Channel, history.com

Because earthquakes aren't traumatic enough on their own, sometimes they come accompanied by something called "earthquake lightning." That's what happens when seismic activity affects certain types of rocks, causing the very ground to appear as if blue, ankle-height flames are shooting up from the depths. It can take a variety of shapes and colors, and the phenomenon has caused people to suspect that they're either experiencing the coming of the Rapture or smack dab in the middle of a hostile alien invasion.

Or a lucky combination of the two, if you happen to be in the right kind of doomsday cult.

> "Bizarre Earthquake Lights Finally Explained," *National Geographic*, nationalgeographic.com

And you can't talk about earthquakes without mentioning tsunamis, right? The relatively recent and devastating tidal waves that struck Japan and Indonesia may have thrust tsunamis into the public consciousness in a major way, but the one that originated in the Indian Ocean in 2004 more than deserves its fame. Set in motion by an immense underwater tremor (with a 9.1 magnitude), the wall of water traveled more than 3,000 miles, annihilating more than 230,000 human lives across fourteen countries.

> ❯ "Ten Years Since the 2004 Indian Ocean Tsunami," *The Atlantic*, theatlantic.com

So now we know that doing "the wave" at sporting events is not only a pretty lame thing to do, it's also in incredibly bad taste, you insensitive bastard.

Fog is creepy enough to have had a crappy movie made about it in 1980 and an even crappier one in 2005. It conjures up images of Jack the Ripper–era London and all manner of Halloween spookiness. But fog also has another way of scaring the pants off you that puts all that other stuff to shame. From time to time a fog bank will form on the ocean and line up so perfectly with the horizon that it can cause onlookers to flee in a panic to high ground, because it looks exactly like an incoming tsunami.

> ❯ "Fog Bank Resembling Tsunami Forms Perfectly in Line with Jersey Shore Coast," ABC News, abcnews.go.com

But once you do realize that you're not going to get hit with a giant wave, at no point do any of the experts explain how exactly you're supposed to deal with all the pirate ghosts.

Massive, yawning craters have been appearing suddenly in an area of Russia known as "the ends of the Earth," and people are starting to panic. That may very well turn out to be an entirely appropriate response too. Scientists blamed the appearance of the craters on global warming, which they say caused the permafrost to melt and methane pockets to explode up from the bowels of the Earth. Whether or not that's the case, if one should happen to blast off in the middle of any of the nearby oilfields, the ensuing explosion might be just as biblical as the locality's nickname.

All things considered, a planet-ending cataclysm that simply involves a bunch of quick explosions is certainly preferable to the inevitable Zombie Robot Apocalypse.

> "The Siberian Crater Saga Is More Widespread—and Scarier—Than Anyone Thought," *Washington Post*, washingtonpost.com

The luckless misfortune of getting fried by a stray lightning bolt probably isn't something you should concern yourself with too much, seeing as how that hardly ever happens to anybody. Everyone should really just relax, and pay no attention whatsoever to the fact that, at any given time, there are 1,800 thunderstorms occurring somewhere on Earth, and 100 lightning strikes per second.

> "Thunderstorms," Weather Explained, weatherexplained.com

So go ahead. Wear a tinfoil tracksuit the next time you go golfing. Climb a church steeple with a car antenna between your teeth. The odds are on your side!

In 2010, the Russian city of St. Petersburg experienced its coldest winter in more than thirty years. There were casualties involved, certainly, but some of the tragedy occurred well after the fact—when falling icicles bludgeoned and impaled several people to death, and caused grievous injuries to dozens.

❯"Falling Icicles Kill Record Numbers in St Petersburg," *Telegraph*, telegraph.co.uk

The number of victims who had their tongues stuck to poles at the time of death may never be known.

When Mongolia experiences a particularly devastating winter it's called a "dzud." The hideously freezing weather conditions that occurred during the last dzud, in 2009–2010, were responsible for the deaths of somewhere in the area of 9.7 million heads of livestock. Some of the casualties came about as a result of starvation, but many cows simply froze to death right where they stood.

A situation that admittedly sounds pretty unpleasant if you're a cow, but pretty convenient if you're in the frozen steak distribution business.

❯"Aid Agencies Brace for Devastating Mongolian 'Dzud' This Winter," Reuters, reuters.com